TOURING
IN
SIKKIM AND TIBET

TOURING IN SIKKIM AND TIBET

DAVID MACDONALD

GYAN

Published by

Gyan Publishing House
5, Ansari Road
Daryaganj, New Delhi-110002
Phone: 011-47034999, 9811692060
E-mail: books@gyanbooks.com

Distribution Network
gyanbooks.com
India, USA, Canada, UK, Australia, France

ISBN : 978-81-212-4133-5 (PB)
First Published, Kalimpong, 1930

2nd Impression 2020

Printed at: Gyan Press, Delhi.

Touring in Skkim and Tibet
Author: David Macdonald

TOURING IN SIKKIM AND TIBET

BY

DAVID MACDONALD
Late British Trade Agent,
Gyantse and Yatung,
Tibet.

Author of
"The Land of the Lama" "Twenty Years in Tibet"
and "Tibetan Folk Tales"

KALIMPONG,
Published by the Author

PREFACE.

In the following pages will be found hints to the intending tourist in the Darjeeling Hills, in Sikkim, and in Tibet. These notes are the result of personal experience of the writer and members of his family, who, resident in Tibet and Sikkim for many years, have experience of practically every possible tour that the visitor is likely to make.

Since the publication of the most recent Guide Book to these Hills, conditions and prices have considerably altered, and these facts, together with repeated requests from friends and travellers who have passed through Kalimpong, form the excuse for the present pamphlet.

Realising that in a volume of the present size many points of interest to the individual must necessarily be omitted, the author wishes to inform any intending tourist that he will be pleased, on request, to give any further information that may be of use in particular cases.

He also takes this opportunity of acknowledging the great assistance he has received, in the editing and production of this guide book, from Mr. F. W. R. Perry of the Himalayan Hotel, Kalimpong.

KALIMPONG, David Macdonald.

July, 1930.

CONTENTS.

	Page.
Preface.	
The Sikkim State.	1
Tibet.	4
The People.	7
Brief Historical Note.	11
Religion.	15
Flora.	19
Fauna, and Lepidoptera.	21
Curios.	23
Touring Information.	24
Specimen Tours.	72
Kalimpong.	79
Detailed Tours.	86
Appendix	

TOURING

IN

SIKKIM AND TIBET

THE SIKKIM STATE.

SIKKIM, or Dejong, as it is known to the neighbouring peoples, is a small protected Native State lying to the north of the Darjeeling District of Bengal.

It forms a wedge between its two larger neighbours, Bhutan and Nepal, on the east and west, while to the north lies the great Tibetan plateau.

Sikkim measures only 65 miles from north to south, and 45 miles from east to west, but within its narrow confines is to be found some of the finest mountain and ravine scenery in the world.

The Kinchenjunga group of mountains alone repays the traveller for his trouble in penetrating to its foot. Everest lies without the boundaries of Sikkim, but is visible from several viewpoints along certain of the recognised tours. From certain vantage points in Sikkim one can gaze on a sheer slope of mountain side some 22000 feet in depth, a gigantic mass of the earth's surface whose feet lie in deep gorges, while its summit pierces the skies.

Within the Sikkim frontiers are experienced climatic conditions ranging from tropical to arctic, with appropriate flora and fauna. On the uplands, the air is clean and fresh, blown straight off the snows, and to the jaded dweller in the steamy plains of India, no finer holiday can be made than an excursion into the heart of these mountains.

Describing a tour made towards the end of the rains, J. Claude White, a former Political Officer in Sikkim, writes:

'The foliage of the trees and the undergrowth is magnificent, most of the flowering shrubs and creepers are at their best, everything looks fresh, and the colouring, when the sun breaks through the clouds, is wonderful. Each leaf and bit of moss sparkles as though set in diamonds, the air is filled with clouds of butterflies of every imaginable colour.

The near distance is brilliant, while the middle and far distances shade in blues and purples to deep indigo, and when a glimpse of the snows is obtained, at the head of some valley, they stand out, an almost supernatural vision of ethereal beauty, the whole picture made up of the softest of tints, not to be equalled in any other part of the world.

The cloud effects are marvellous, the vapour seems to boil up out of the deep valleys, as out of some huge cauldron, taking the most fantastic shapes, and an endless variety of colours as it catches the sun's rays. Then suddenly everything is blotted out into a monotonous grey, as though such sights were too grand for human eyes, until a sudden puff of wind blows aside the veil of mist, and discloses again the lovely panorama.'

Sikkim, owing to the proximity of the great Kinchenjunga range, and the lie of its innumerable valleys, experiences a very wet rainy season, the fall varying from 60 inches in the north, to over 200 inches per annum in the south. Darjeeling has an annual rainfall of 120 inches, Kalimpong only 80.

Sikkim is drained by the river Teesta and its tributaries, in fact it is nothing more than the catchment area for this river system. The chief affluents of the Teesta are the Lachen and Lachung, which join to form the main river, the Rungeet, which forms the Sikkim-Darjeeling frontier, and the Rongni.

The valley of the Teesta is magnificent, a deep cut gorge, called by some visitors the 'Trossachs of the Himalayas'. This river, when in flood, is a wonderful and awe-inspiring sight.

The mountain system which forms Sikkim consists of two great spurs, jutting out from the main watershed of the Himalayas, which lies actually within Tibet. These two spurs, known as the Chola and the Singelela on the east and the west respectively, run roughly from north to south; and are more or less parallel.

They themselves are again cut up into innumerable cross valleys, running in every conceivable direction, each valley having its own drainage stream. In the rains, some of these small side streams become raging torrents, but as soon as the rain stops they quickly resume their normal size.

A peculiarity of this part of the Himalayas is that there are no dunes or low foot hills. The mountains run abruptly down to the plains, and then stop short. A very good example of this is to be seen at Sevoke, a station on the Teesta Valley Extension of the Darjeeling Himalayan Railway. Here the Teesta suddenly debouches on to the Dooars, literally 'Doors', the famous tea district of Bengal. At this spot, even when within a few hundred yards of the plains, one has no conception of their proximity.

TIBET.

TIBET is an absolutely different country from Sikkim, as regards scenery. The Chumbi Valley, of course, lying on the southern side of the great Himalayan Divide, presents much the same physical characteristics as Sikkim, to which country, geographically speaking, it belongs.

Once on the plateau, however, the scene is completely changed. Wooded slopes and deep valleys give place to a series of flat basin-like plains, obviously old lake beds, separated by low ranges of weathered hills. These latter, of course, are low only in comparison with the plains they border.

Along the trade route followed by the tourist, however, the eye is held for several days of the march by the immense mountain mass of Chomolhari, the Queen of the Divine Hills, a mountain sacred to all Tibetans.

The fascination of Tibet lies in its utter bleakness and wildness, and also in its, at present, unspoiled and unsophisticated people.

Once the traveller has climbed on to the plateau, not a bush, let alone a tree, breaks the monotony of the windswept plains, until he reaches the town of Gyantse. Only a few stunted willows are to be found in sheltered places, where they are prized as providing wind-breaks to the local people when the latter are picnicking, a form of diversion of which the Tibetans are very fond.

THE PEOPLE.

THE earliest known inhabitants of the Darjeeling District and Sikkim were the Lepchas, or Rong, the 'ravine folk', as they style themselves.

Their origin is obscure, but they are of pronounced Mongolian type, and some authorities state that they probably migrated in very early times from Assam or Burma.

At the present day they number only some six or seven thousand, and are gradually growing less, owing to their being ousted from their native forests by the more pushful Nepalese cultivator, who is immigrating from Nepal into Sikkim in ever increasing numbers. The Nepalese, being a cultivator, is responsible for the deforestation which is driving the Lepcha out. A peculiar trait of the Nepalese is that he can never resist felling a tree, wherever it may be, if excuse offers.

The Lepchas are of a shy retiring nature, preferring to live in out of the way jungles and forests. They are improvident, and greatly addicted to strong liquor, which, like other hill-tribes, they brew from locally grown millet.

Every Lepcha is a born naturalist, and living as they do in the forests, they know the habits of every beast and bird, and make first-rate collectors. They have a name for every living thing, including plants, which is found in their country.

As private servants, especially as cooks, they excel, provided they can keep from the bottle, and many of them, especially in the Darjeeling District, have taken up this kind of work.

Though outwardly professing Buddhism, they are at heart confirmed animists, worshipping the spirits of mountain, forest and river. Small in stature and seemingly not robust, yet they have immense powers of endurance and are tireless on the march.

Nowadays, the great bulk of the people of the Darjeeling District are Nepalese, with a sprinkling of what may be called Darjeeling Tibetans, Lepchas, and Sherpas, the former being the descendants of refugees at various times from Tibet.

In Sikkim the upper classes and the landed proprietors, known as Kazis, are mainly of Tibetan origin, the royal family of the State also hailing from that country. The first king was, it is true, Lepcha, but constant intermarriage with Tibetans, from among whom the Maharaja always selects his bride, has practically eliminated all trace of the original Lepcha blood. In Sikkim also, as already mentioned, the great bulk of the inhabitants are Nepalese immigrants.

It is a regrettable fact that most of these are in the hands of the Marwaries, who seem to penetrate everywhere where there is anything to be made out of money-lending. One sees them even in the Trade Marts of Tibet, although they are not at present tolerated in Lhasa itself.

The Nepalese, indeed, all the hill people, are notoriously improvident, and for immediate accommodation in money matters, will pledge their property at most exorbitant rates of interest. Marriages, celebration of puja, and such like occasions are when the unfortunate cultivator falls into the hands of the Jews of India.

At present, the policy of Tibet for the Tibetans, is strictly enforced, and other nationals are not allowed to own land therein. Nepalese traders have, however, of recent years been getting more and more hold on the petty trade of the larger towns. The wool trade, the most important item in exports from Tibet, is largely in the hands of the Marwaries, who finance the various Tibetan wool-dealers.

While Sikkim is possibly not so priest-ridden as Tibet, owing to the large number of Nepalese in the former country, yet even there the Lamas wield considerable influence, both in the conduct of State affairs, and among the Buddhist, or rather Lamaist section of the people. They play on the intense superstition of their ignorant and child-like followers, and in many things, completely control the latter.

BRIEF HISTORICAL NOTE.

SIKKIM was settled by the Lepchas at some time prior to the twelfth century A. D. The present ruling dynasty, claiming descent from Thri Srong De Tsan, one of the most famous of Tibetan warrior kings, who ruled in pre-Lamaist days, gained their powers somewhen around 1300 A. D.

1641 saw their conversion, by missionary lamas from Tibet, to Buddhism, and the then chief, or gyalpo, was consecrated as king.

The present Maharaja, Sir Tashi Namgyal, K. C. I. E., is the eleventh in direct descent from this first consecrated king.

In the years 1700-1706, Sikkim was overrun by the Bhutanese, who were only expelled with Tibetan aid, and from that time, up to 1888, the latter Power exercised great influence at the Court of her small neighbour. Towards the end of the eighteenth century, Sikkim was again invaded, this time by the Gurkhas, who stripped from her what is now the Nepalese province of Limbuana, besides certain other territory.

Following aggression in Tibet, however, in 1792, the Nepalese were defeated by a Chinese army, called to their aid by the Tibetans, and Sikkim received some of her lands back, but not all. During this invasion of Tibet, the Gurkhas sacked Shigatse, the second city of the Lamas, but were forced later to conclude a humiliating peace outside the walls of their capital Khatmandu.

Sikkim, however, continued to pay tribute to Nepal until 1815, and only after the defeat of the Gurkhas by the British in that year, were the Terai and Western Sikkim finally handed back to their rightful owners, the Sikkim Raj.

Internecine quarrelling, and acts of hostility towards British subjects, culminating in the arrest and ill-treatment of Messrs. Hooker and Campbell, brought retribution at various times in the form of annexation of territory by the Government of India. Thus was the present Darjeeling District acquired, though in the beginning, the sanitarium of Darjeeling was opened on land rented from the Sikkim Raj.

In 1861, Sikkimese territory was limited by treaty to north of the Rungeet, though it was not until 1888, however, that Sikkim was brought into the position of a protected Native State, and the influence of Tibet within her borders finally eradicated. This was brought about by the penetration of a Tibetan force into Sikkimese territory to a place called Lingtu, below Gnatong, where the remains of their fort are still to be seen. Refusal to withdraw, and to recognise the Sikkim boundaries established by a Frontier Commission, brought down on the Tibetans a force despatched by the Government of India, which drove them from Lingtu, across the Jelap Pass, and down into the Chumbi Valley.

Since that time, relations between Sikkim and the Government of India have been cordial, especially of recent years.

Association with India has been of the greatest benefit to Sikkim and to her people, who are secured from invasion and annexation by her neighbours, and assured of peace. The development of the country, though this will naturally be slow, has been begun by the opening up of better communications.

As a matter of fact, owing to transport difficulties, Sikkim can never become really wealthy, but British administration has saved her from a state of complete insolvency.

Nowadays, all internal affairs have been handed over to the Maharaja, while its foreign relations only are controlled by the Government of India. The latter has, since 1888, stationed a Political Officer at Gangtok, the capital.

TIBET.

RELATIONS between India and Tibet were, up to 1912, hampered by the presence of China as the suzerain power in the latter country. The Chinese were mainly responsible for the policy of isolation adopted by Tibet, which was only broken by the penetration of the Younghusband Mission to Lhasa in 1904, and the treaty resulting therefrom.

From 1904 up to 1925, the Tibetans, once the Chinese had been driven from their country in 1912, became very friendly towards the British, but of recent years, their attitude has not been so cordial, for several reasons, for the detailing of which the present volume does not afford scope.

Tibet is ruled by the Dalai Lama, assisted by a council of four Chief Ministers, or Shap-pes, and a Prime Minister, or Lonchen. Local administration is in the hands of Jongpens, or District Magistrates, the trade route over which European visitors travel being jointly administered by British and Tibetan Trade Agents.

The history of Tibet is too involved to detail in this work, but those interested will find an account in my book, the 'Land of the Lama'.

RELIGION.

THE state religion of both Sikkim and Tibet is Lamaism, a form of Buddhism. Lamaism has travelled far from the faith laid down by Gautama Buddha, and is now a combination of Hinduism and Animism with very little of the pure faith left. The bulk of the Nepalese profess Hinduism, a few being Buddhists, and these latter are spiritually subject to the Lamaist Church.

Prominent features of the countryside in Sikkim and Tibet are the numerous gompas, or monasteries. These are almost invariably situated in the most picturesque and commanding positions, wherever possible, on the face of a mountain slope.

Religion enters very largely into the everyday life of the people, and they have lavished much time and skill on the interior decoration of some of their temples, while valuable altar vessels and silken hangings testify to the generosity of pious Lamaists.

Tibetan monasteries are, as a rule, larger than those in Sikkim, in which state the most important is that of Pemayangtse. This institution, which only accepts candidates for the priesthood from the upper classes, is, unfortunately, very modern in appearance, its beauty being marred by a corrugated iron roof, a testimony to the march of progress in the Himalayas!

The lamas of this place, while not refusing admittance to European visitors, are not as courteous as those of other gompas, especially in Tibet, probably because they are too sophisticated where tourists are concerned. They also expect a large monetary present from visitors, and produce a book in which former donations are noted as an inducement to subscribe.

It may be noted here that certain of the frescoes in Pemayangtse monastery are not of the kind to shew a Sunday school class, being Tantric, and consequently suggestive of immorality.

Monasteries were, according to the Lamaist precepts, originally built in out of the way places, but in the course of years, considerable villages have grown up around most of the more important ones, especially in Sikkim.

The maintainance of the monasteries forms a great drag on the lay portion of the population, for the lamas are non-productive, and have to be fed and clothed by their lay fellow-countrymen. In Tibet, no less than one-sixth of the adult male population are priests. The people put up with this state of affairs partly on account of their superstition, and partly because practically every family in the land has at least one member a lama.

Monastery buildings usually conform to a more or less standard design, consisting of a main hall for worship, containing the altar and library, with a porch, in which are to be found the effigies of the Four Guardian Kings of the quarters. In the larger institutions numerous side chapels open off the main temple hall.

The dwellings of the lamas are grouped around the central building, lay followers being housed outside the temple compound proper, in small godowns. Some monasteries are single, others double-storied. A prominent feature of many of them is a huge prayer wheel placed in the porch, sometimes containing millions of prayers, which ascend heavenwards at each revolution. Occasionally one sees the sacred number of 108 small prayer-wheels placed round the outer wall of the main hall. Pious Lamaists walk round the building in the proper direction, with the wall on the right, and turn these in order to acquire merit.

One frequently comes across a sacred edifice called a choten, fashioned from hewn stone or plaster, usually whitewashed. These choten, sometimes containing sacred books or relics, are erected by pious people either in the hope of acquiring spiritual merit, or as a penance for past misdeeds.

Choten are always built in five sections, each section representing one of the five Lamaist elements.

Commencing from the top these elements are, Ether, Air, Fire, Water, and Earth.

The long walls, or mendong, seen in the middle of the paths, are another expression of faith on the part of the Lamaists. These walls, carrying along their sides slabs on which are inscribed the sacred formula *"Om! Mani Padme Hum!"* (Hail! Jewel in the Lotus!), must be passed with the right hand next to them.

Surrounding many of the monasteries and larger private residences will be seen lofty poles to which are attached long strips of printed cloth.

These are the famous prayer flags, and every time they flutter in the wind, the prayers inscribed thereon are wafted to the Gods, for the benefit of the person whose name is inscribed thereon. It is a merit gaining act to erect these flags, and the merit is increased if the sacred number of 108 are put up.

Prayer flags, consisting merely of tiny slips of paper or cloth will be seen on the passes, placed there to propitiate the spirits of the storm and mountains, and to ensure safe passage for those who tie them there.

FLORA.

THE flora of Sikkim and the Chumbi Valley is exceptionally varied. One finds plants, flowers, and trees of every kind from the sub-tropical to the arctic. In the higher valleys tiny wild flowers form a literal carpet to the feet, in the Spring. In the Chumbi Valley the hillsides are clothed with wild dog-roses, pines, firs, larches, and spruce.

These hills are a botanist's paradise, and there is always the chance of finding a rare orchid or primula. In this connection it should be noted that orchids may not be exported from Sikkim without the permission of the Sikkim Durbar.

The chief feature of northern Sikkim is the rhododendron, which clothes the mountain sides below 12000 feet with masses of colour. Each slope seems to have its own particular shade of flowers, which are carried on trees and shrubs ranging from forty feet to only a few inches in height, the plant getting smaller as the elevation increases. May is the best month in which to see the rhododendron.

Bamboos are present in many varieties, and the Lepchas state that they can tell the elevation of a place from the size of the bamboos found thereat. On the passes one may gather edelweiss without even taking the trouble to descend from the saddle, it is so common.

Tibet proper has little in the way of vegetation beyond arctic plants and mosses. A few flowers may be seen during the brief summer, and of these only the tiny blossom appears above the soil, there being no time nor nourishment for the development of foliage. Even grass seems scarce on the Plateau, and it is amazing how even on this the Tibetan sheep put on fat. The Tibetans themselves say that even though the grass is scanty, yet its powers of nourishment are very great, and indeed, this must be the case.

FAUNA AND LEPIDOPTERA.

INSECT life is most prolific in Sikkim, especially moths and butterflies, of which over 2000 and over 600 species respectively have been catalogued. These butterflies are very brilliantly coloured, especially those found at low elevations, where they fly above the paths in literal clouds. Some are found even on the snowfields, though on what the caterpillar feeds remains a mystery. In the course of even a short tour, an interesting collection may be made by the enthusiast. The best spots are in the warm valleys, near water, and the best time just after the rains, say October.

At certain times of the year, in Sikkim, the cicadas become a nuisance, and their noise is deafening, and must be heard to be believed.

Tibet also has its insect life, butterflies and moths and so forth, though they are comparatively rare.

Sikkim is not a sportsman's country, game is not numerous, except in the north, although the birds are said to number several hundred species. It is strange that one does not see much in the way of bird life when touring, at any rate along the roads.

The absence of game is probably accounted for by the presence, in the rains, of pests such as the leech and the tick, which infest the jungles for five months of the year. Northern Sikkim and Tibet are the habitat of the big wild sheep, and also of the gazelle, Tibetan stag, and the Burrhel.

For Sikkim, permission to shoot may be obtained from the Sikkim Darbar, but is impossible to obtain for Tibet, where shooting is absolutely forbidden to visitors. Rules governing sport in Sikkim are attached for reference.

Shooting and fishing permits for the Darjeeling District are obtainable from the Secretary, Darjeeling Shooting and Fishing Association, at a cost of Rs. 30/- for both sports, and application should be made to this official.

CURIOS.

TO those intending to purchase curios a word of advice is necessary unless they happen to be authorities on the art of this part of the Himalayas.

Unless specimens are obtained from a reputable dealer, the visitor is very likely to be swindled badly. Especially is this the case in Darjeeling, which town is getting an unenviable reputation for fakes. Purchases are better made in Kalimpong, where the author is prepared to advise collectors as to the genuineness and value of their purchases. Prices in Kalimpong also run somewhat lower than elsewhere, at present. It is of course understood that the above refers to valuable curios, and not to the cheap souvenirs sold by the roadside.

No fixed rate can be laid down as to prices, experience alone can guide.

TOURING INFORMATION.

TOURING in the Darjeeling District, in Sikkim and in Tibet nowadays presents no difficulties, at least to the person who possesses average health. Those who are at all troubled with heart should on no account attempt to visit the higher elevation places. Most parts of these countries are served with excellent roads or bridle paths, and anyone, even ladies unaccompanied by their men-folk, need have no fears as to their personal safety, or that of their baggage.

It is in the writer's opinion, far safer for unattended ladies to travel in Sikkim and Tibet, than in British India. Wherever one goes, the local people shew unfailing courtesy and helpfulness, should occasion arise.

Travellers are permitted, provided the necessary passes are forthcoming, to travel anywhere in Sikkim while for the Darjeeling District no permission is required. In Tibet, the farthest point to which the ordinary visitor may penetrate is Gyantse, a Trade Mart, the headquarters of a British Trade Agent, and his military escort. When visiting this city, tourists must not leave the main Kalimpong, Pharijong, Gyantse route, without special permission.

It may be mentioned here that this special permission which can only be granted by the Government of India, is very seldom given. Protection can only be given while travellers of British Nationality are on the official trade route, travel on this being secured by the Trade Regulations of 1908.

SEASONS FOR TOURING.

AS regards the Darjeeling District and Sikkim, in which weather conditions are much the same, it is pleasant touring at any time during the cold weather and just after the rains. July and August are bad months, when travel, except in the north of Sikkim, is unpleasant, for several reasons. Among these are the risk of getting one's kit soaked through day after day, and the presence of the jungle pests, of which the leech alone, met with between 4000 and 10000 feet, renders life almost unbearable to man and beast, making it impossible to leave the beaten track even for a few yards. Excessive rainfall causes slips on the roads and tracks, while small bridges are washed away by the side streams coming down in spate. Ticks are a nuisance during the monsoon, at low elevations, and at that time the mosquitos are at their worst.

The best times for touring in these parts are the months of October, November and December, the later the better. At this time one is assured of clear fine weather, magnificent views, and cool days and nights. After December, although the weather is fine, it is very cold in the high elevation bungalows, and the views are marred by the haze, partly due to dust, partly to the smoke of numerous small forest fires, while banking snow-clouds obscure the heights.

Moreover, at high elevations, snow may block the roads, and in some cases render touring on certain routes impossible.

From December, however, until the rains break, touring may be done in the southern part of Sikkim, but low elevation and valley bungalows should as far as possible be avoided. Heat in the narrow gorges is most oppressive, and mosquitos and flies are a nuisance.

Touring in the Darjeeling District may be done even in the rains, as owing to the broader roads and paths the pests are not so troublesome as in Sikkim.

For northern Sikkim and Tibet the best months are April to October, especially as the monsoon does not cross the main Himalayan divide. The rhododendrons are at their best in May in the Pass country, which one must traverse to reach Tibet, though snow may be experienced as late as the end of April.

The Chumbi Valley in June is lovely, the climate being that of an English Spring, with lanes of wild roses, and a carpet of primulas, irises, cowslips, and innumerable other small wild flowers.

In the winter the cold in Tibet is intense, and the wind, which invariably blows a gale, is very bitter. Duststorms also render travel the reverse of pleasant.

FRONTIER PASSES.

FRONTIER passes must be obtained by all intending visitors to Sikkim and Tibet. Those for Sikkim are issued by the Deputy Commissioner of Darjeeling, to whom application should be made at least a fortnight before the date of the commencement of the tour.

It has recently been made a general rule that Sikkim passes should be applied for in person, and if possible, this should be done. Where it is not convenient, however, a letter of identification, signed by some government official, or prominent person, should occompany the letter of application. This should obviate any delay that might otherwise occur in the issue of the passes.

These precautions have been rendered necessary owing to several travellers having forced their way past the frontier guards without passes, on some pretext or other, or to their not having observed the conditions under which these passes are granted.

Nowadays, without the production of a current frontier pass, no person will be allowed to enter Sikkim or Tibet on any pretext whatever.

When applying for frontier passes, a fee of As. 8/- per person should be forwarded to the Deputy

Commissioner, Darjeeling, by money order, not in stamps, and a note to the effect that this has been done made in the letter of application. The following information should be supplied.

1. Dates between which passes are required.

2. Proposed route. (Unless previous sanction has been obtained, this route must be adhered to).

Sikkim passes are granted subject to the grantee giving his written promise that he will abide by the following conditions. That he will not shoot or fish without permission; and that he will not cross the frontiers of Tibet, Nepal or Bhutan without further permission from the Government of India.

Application for passes to enter Tibet should be made to the Political Officer in Sikkim, at least two months previous notice being advisable, personal information similar to that given for Sikkim being also supplied. The purpose for which entry is asked, such as pleasure, should also be stated.

Visitors to Tibet must possess both Sikkim and Tibet frontier passes. No fee is charged for Tibet passes, which as a rule are granted for a period extending only up to six weeks from the date of crossing the Tibet frontier to the date of recrossing the same.

RESTHOUSES AND DAK BUNGLOWS.

ELSEWHERE is given a full list, with all necessary details, of resthouses and dak-bungalows in which accommodation is available for tourists. The fees, payable in advance, are Rs. 2 per person per day and night, (24 hours). Passes for the use of these bungalows must be obtained before starting on the tour. Fees for Tibet bungalows are Re. 1/- per person, per 24 hrs. Passes for these are issued by the Political Officer in Sikkim, Gangtok, Sikkim.

In the unforeseen event of a halt being made at a bungalow for which passes have not been obtained, double rates, viz. Rs. 4 must be paid to the chowkidar, and a note to this effect made in the Visitors' Book.

Where there are no dak-bungalows, no charge is made for the use of camping grounds.

Bungalow passes are granted subject to certain conditions, which are shewn in the accompanying schedule, and which should be scrupulously observed.

The same rules as laid down for Sikkim Bungalows apply to those in Tibet. All breakages must be paid for at the time of the visit at rates laid down and hung in each bungalow, a note being made in the Visitors' Book.

Each bungalow is looked after by a chowkidar, as a rule a very obliging individual, ready to help in any way he can. He must not, however, be looked on as an extra private servant, as he is appointed solely to care for the property left in his charge in the bungalow, and to see that no unauthorised person occupies it, and that rules are observed. Chowkidars usually provide firewood, and milk, while they are sometimes willing to sell eggs, fowls, and so forth to travellers.

Should he have proved attentive, a tip, of say As. 4 per person in the party, may be given, with a maximum of Re. 1.

Bungalows in Sikkim and Tibet are fully furnished, those above 7000 feet elevation being provided with mattresses also. Forest and Khas Mahal resthouses in the Darjeeling District are sparely furnished, and have little in the way of cooking utensils or cutlery and crockery.

CENTRES FOR TOURING.

FOR most of the tours Kalimpong affords the most suitable starting point. In this town, transport, servants, stores, and all to do with touring, may be arranged much cheaper than in Darjeeling, and most important of all, mules can be readily obtained for the carriage of kit. They are more satisfactory than coolies or ponies.

The Himalayan Hotel, in Kalimpong, caters specially for tourists in the hills and in Tibet, and the Proprietors, who have lived for years in Tibet and the Darjeeling District, can advise intending travellers, on receipt of enquiry, from their own experience.

They can give letters of introduction to Sikkimese and Tibetan notables and officials and prominent people, and thus afford visitors experiences which would otherwise be missed. They will make all arrangements for either short or long tours, with or without guides and interpreters. All the intending tourist need do is to take his ticket to Siliguri and the Himalayan Hotel will do the rest.

The other centre for touring, Darjeeling, is convenient for the Sandakphu-Phalut trip. In this town arrangements for tourists will be made by the

Sirdars attached to the various Hotels. These men will engage servants, riding animals, and coolies, and will charge about Rs. 4 per day for their services. They accompany the traveller on tour.

For those tourists who may be pressed for time, it is now possible, except during and immediately after the rains, to motor direct from Siliguri to Gantok, the capital of Sikkim, where they can pick up their servants, etc., and commence their tour. As mentioned above, the Proprietors of the Himalayan Hotel, will, if required, make all these arrangements, including cars from Siliguri, the cost of which, to Gantok, will be approximately Rs. 70/- per car. Several days may thus be saved and the traveller can get farther afield.

SERVANTS.

UNLESS the traveller already has in his employ men who are hillmen, and used to touring in out of the way places, it is advisable to leave all permanent servants behind, when on tour in Sikkim and Tibet. Should they be taken, they usually fall sick in some out of the way place, and become a burden, instead of a help. Moreover, they do not know the places and people along the roads, as do the regular touring servants, who are constantly up and down the countryside. Plains' servants, also, do not get on too well with the hill-peoples.

The best course is to engage all the necessary tour personnel in the place from which a start is being made, through some reliable agency which can vouch for their honesty and capabilities.

For two people the following servants are sufficient.

1 Cook on Rs. 3. per day.
1 Bearer on Rs. 2/8/- per day.
1 Sweeper on Rs. 1/8/- per day.

These rates are those prevailing at Kalimpong at the time of writing. If economy is a consideration, one man can be engaged for a party of not more than two, who will combine the duties of cook and bearer. In such cases he will require Rs. 4/- per day. Parties of more than two should always take a separate cook and bearer.

The duties of the cook are explained by his title, while the bearer should be responsible for packing and unpacking, bed making, service at table, and generally looking after the comfort of his employers. The sweeper, in addition to looking after the bathrooms, should sweep up the rooms that have been occupied in each Dak Bungalow, before the party leaves. He will also prepare food for any dogs that may be taken along. For rough work, such as carrying bath water, and so forth, the tiffin coolie may be used, or if a tiffin coolie is not taken, a local man may usually be obtained, who will do the work for a few annas in the shape of a tip.

TRANSPORT.

ALL articles taken on the tour, such as bedding, store boxes, suitcases, etc., etc., are carried from halt to halt either by animals or coolies. Wherever the roads, and especially the bridges permit, mules are by far the best means of transport in every way. They are quicker and more reliable than coolies, besides being cheaper.

Coolies should only be taken when mules are not available, as sometimes happens in Darjeeling, or when the tour takes the traveller into western or northern Sikkim, where the bamboo bridges will not carry animal traffic.

A tiffin coolie, however, is always useful, for carrying small articles that may be required on the march, and for carrying the lunch basket. He keeps with the tourist party wherever they go, and also helps in the bungalow at the end of the stage. Waterproofs should be carried strapped to the saddle.

Pack animals carry a load of one maund on either side and this weight should not be exceeded when making up the various packages. Coolies should not be loaded with more than 50 lbs per man. No allowance need be made for mule or pony rations, this being the concern of the owner of the animals, who makes his own arrangements.

Servants' baggage and coolies' kit and rations must be carried at their employers' expense. One maund weight should suffice for this when animal transport is taken, while one coolie in eight should be allotted for the same purpose.

On marches which go over 12000 feet, and always in Tibet, it is advisable to mount the cook and the bearer, as otherwise they lag behind, and do not reach the bungalows ahead of their employers, as is necessary if comfort is desired.

With mule transport, as the loads grow lighter owing to consumption of food, animals become available for mounting the servants without engaging extra mules.

For riding purposes mules or ponies are available, and there is little to choose between them. Mules if anything have the preference.

It is not advisable for people straight up from the Plains to undertake a purely walking tour, for should sore feet result, or stiffness set in or the effect of strenuous exercise at great heights affect the heart, the entire pleasure of the trip may be spoiled. A good plan is to walk down hill and if inclined, along the level, and to ride up hill. On some of the tours one climbs several thousand feet in the course of a few miles, and assistance for these places is really necessary.

Pack mules are hired out in teams of from six to ten animals, and each team is in charge of two muleteers. In the writer's opinion mules are more satisfactory than ponies for riding purposes, the only objection being that no separate syce is sent with each riding mule. Should it become necessary, however, to have the mules held during a halt, the tiffin coolie can do this. If travellers bring their own saddlery, it should be remembered that the mules and ponies are small, seldom over twelve hands, and that cruppers are necessary, as they have little in the way of withers to prevent the saddle from slipping forward on down grades.

Rates for transport are as below:—

Riding pony ...	...	Rs. 5 per stage.
Riding mule ...	...	Rs. 3 to Rs. 3/8/- per stage.
Pack mule ...	...	Rs. 2 to Rs. 2/8/- per stage.
Coolie ...	...	Rs. 1/4/- per stage.

The government coolies that are mentioned in other guidebooks as obtainable at As. 10 and As. 12 per day are not satisfactory. Application for these is made through the local authorities, and the various villages have to supply the men, who do not go further than one stage from their homes. Such labour is practically forced, and delay always occurs in collecting the coolies at each stage.

CLOTHING.

LITTLE extra in the way of clothing beyond what the traveller already possesses is necessary, except in the depth of winter in northern Sikkim. Plenty of bedding should be taken, as one can be miserable if cold at night. Sheets make for comfort and should be taken.

A sufficient supply of clean underclothing should be included, enough for six to ten days, and on long tours a day's halt should occasionally be made to enable clothes to be washed.

While the days may be warm, even hot, the night temperatures are cool, and a warm suit or dress should be taken into which one can change on arrival at the end of the days march. The following list may be of use as a guide in the selection of clothing for a ten days' tour.

For a man.

4 Pairs Khaki Shorts.
4 Khaki Shirts.
8 Pairs Stockings.
2 Pairs woollen Socks.
1 Pair Puttees.
1 Pair Heavy walking Shoes.
1 Pair Comfortable Ammunition Boots.

2 Warm Vests.
2 Light Vests.
1 Pair Riding Breeches, or Jodhpurs.
1 Sports Coat.
1 Pair Grey Flannel Trousers.
1 Blazer.
1 Tie.
2 Pairs Warm Drawers.
1 Cap or tweed hat.
1 Topee.
1 Muffler.
1 Pullover.
2 Pairs Pyjamas.
1 Dressing Gown.
1 Waterproof.
1 Pair Slippers.
1 Pair Warm Gloves.
Handkerchiefs,
Toilet Requisites.
Towels, etc., etc.,

For a Lady.

1 Riding Suit.
2 Pairs Walking Shoes.
1 Pair Slippers.
1 Warm Skirt and Jumper.
2 Sets warm undies.
3 Sets Silk or Cotton undies.
4 Pairs Warm Stockings:
2 Washing Frocks.

1 Topee.
1 Soft Felt Hat.
1 Dressing Gown.
3 Nightdresses or Pyjamas.
1 Pair Warm Gloves.
1 Muffler.
Towels,
Toilet Requisites.
Handkerchiefs etc., etc.,

In the warmer weather, shorts and khaki shirts are being used more and more by lady travellers, and if desired, a supply of these may be taken.

For the heights, for winter, and for travelling in Tibet, where the wind is trying, the following additions should be made.

1 Warm Greatcoat.
1 Extra Set very Warm Underclothing.
1 Warm Tweed Suit.

A leather coat is very useful on the Tibetan Plateau as a protection from the wind, and a hot water bottle of the rubber variety should be included for those who suffer from cold feet at night.

The following bedding should be taken for most tours, two extra blankets being added for Tibet and northern Sikkim.

2 Pillows
4 Pillow Cases.
4 Sheets.
4 Blankets.
1 Rezai or Camp Mattress.

Mattresses are, as has already been mentioned, supplied in the higher elevation bungalows, but where they are not, a rezai is indispensable for comfort.

A mosquito net should be taken along for use when halts are made in low elevation bungalows during the warmer months, April-July.

Sleeping bags are useful in very cold places, and when one is under canvas.

On long tours, where halts are made for washing clothes, a small flat iron makes for extra comfort. It weighs only a few pounds, and is well worth carrying along for the pleasure an ironed handkerchief or sheet gives as opposed to the plain dried variety. The traveller will probably have to do his or her own ironing, but it is well worth the trouble.

LAMPS AND STOVES.

LAMPS are provided in practically every bungalow, but kerosene oil for these must be carried by the tourist. Oil is procurable in all the larger bazaars, but not in the smaller villages.

It is therefore advisable to carry a petrol tin full of kerosene, which can be replenished as occasion arises. Such a tin will not leak, is handy for loading, and is not too heavy. A few packets of candles, the carriage variety are the best, should be packed for use in emergencies, while a couple of hurricane lanterns will be found to be useful in the kitchen, as well as on the road should the party be benighted. Electric torches, with spare batteries, should be carried.

A most useful article on tour is a Primus stove, or better still, a stove burning solid fuel, such as Meta, as the former requires methylated spirits to get it going. On arrival in a bungalow, when hot water for tea is required quickly, and the servants are late, a portable stove is a boon.

STORE AND RATION.

TRAVELLERS unused to Sikkim usually make the mistake of carrying too much tinned provisions. For Tibet these are necessary, as one can obtain nothing on the road, but in Sikkim, almost all ordinary bazaar supplies are available *en route* at the various bazaars.

Fowls, eggs, rice, potatoes, and other vegetables, flour, sugar, oil, are all obtainable locally along most of the routes. Prepared tinned food is of course, very convenient at times, but wherever possible, fresh rations should be prepared.

All bazaar supplies can be obtained at the following places, also, as a rule, fresh meat.

Kalimpong, Darjeeling, Pedong, Rhenock, Rongli, Yatung, Pharijong, Gyantse, Gantok, Rangpo, Algarah. Store boxes can be filled up as one passes through the various bazaars.

Breakfast and dinner can always be freshly cooked, and often there is no need to carry an elaborate lunch for the road. Ham sandwiches, hard boiled eggs, cheese, biscuits, chocolate, and such like articles will afford a sufficient variety for roadside tiffins, and there will always be some cold meat remaining from dinner that can be utilised.

Most of the marches will be covered in five hours or so, even allowing halts for photography, lunch, etc.

Tinned and preserved stores, if purchased in Calcutta, should be packed in boxes not exceding one maund, 80 lbs, in weight, including packing, instructions being given to the packers to place the stores in hinged boxes fitted with hasps for padlocks. For coolie transport the weight will of course be less. The hinged lids, though a trifle more expensive, are much more satisfactory than nailed boxes, the lids of which, after being opened two or three times, fall to pieces. With locked boxes, moreover, a check can be kept on expenditure, necessary articles being issued daily to the cook, and the boxes relocked.

In Sikkim and Tibet, fresh milk, when obtainable, should always be boiled before use, and the same remark applies to the water. In no circumstances should travellers drink from wayside streams, no matter how clear and crystal-like they may appear. The chances are that they are polluted higher up, out of sight, and in any case, unless precipitated by alum, their mica content is so great as to upset the internal economy of those unused to the hill water. Below are suggestions for tinned and preserved stores for a party of four for a ten day tour.

2 tins Quaker Oats.	10 small Tins Milk.
4 lbs. Table Butter.	Condiments to taste.
2 lbs Tea.	Sauces and Pickles to taste.
5 lbs Sugar.	2 doz Matches.

1 Cooked Ham.
1 Tin Cocoa.
10 Slabs Chocolate.
2 lbs Cheese.
1 Tin Arrowroot.
Cakes, (tinned).

3 lbs Jam.
2 lbs Marmalade.
4 Tins biscuits.
½ lb Macaroni.
4 doz. Soup cubes.
or
Sufficient Campbells Soups.

Meats, Tinned Fruits, and Drinks according to taste.

A supply of bread can be taken from the starting point and after it is finished, the cook will make substitutes in the form of unsweetened scones, rolls, etc.

TOBACCO.

SMOKERS should take a supply sufficient for their tour of their favourite tobacco or cigarettes, as once away from Kalimpong or Darjeeling, there will be no chance to obtain more till the return. None but the cheapest and commonest brands of cigarettes are to be bought en route.

These cheap smokes can be bought for the staff, and each member given a packet after the day's march is over.

MARCHES.

MARCHES should not be too long. A good average is 12 to 15 miles per day, rather less if the road is largely up and down, and the bungalows are placed at intervals suitable for these distances. The first day's march should be short, as there it always delay in starting on the first morning. Loads have to be arranged and portioned out, mules and coolies have a habit of arriving later than ordered, and it will be found that the 12 miles will be quite long enough for this first day.

As mentioned elsewhere, wherever possible, mule transport should be used, not alone by reason of its cheapness and quickness, but also because the Tibetan muleteers are not so prone to succumb to the attractions of wayside hostelries, as are coolies, if not carefully herded past them.

When actually on the tour, travellers should rise as early as possible, say by six a. m. not on account of the transport alone, but because the early morning affords the finest and clearest views.

As soon as his employers are up, the bearer can pack everything except the food required for breakfast, prepare any sandwiches or such like that are required for lunch or the march, fill thermos flasks, and bring shaving water, etc., While the cook is preparing breakfast, the pack animals and coolies can feed, and as soon as breakfast is over, they can get away with the kit. Before the cook and bearer leave the bungalow, the chowkidars account should be taken in their presence, and paid off. Care should be taken that the bungalow is left clean.

After the servants and luggage have left, it is wise to spend an hour or so exploring the vicinity, in order that they may get well ahead. The tiffin coolie will, of course, remain with his masters.

As regards riding ponies, it is wise to insist that they are fed in front of their employers. This can conveniently be done while waiting for breakfast, and after tea. A full pony ration should consist of at least six pounds weight of Indian Corn, or similar grain, and fourteen pounds of dry grass per day, divided into two feeds.

If one does not see the animals fed, the syces, usually small boys, will surely fail to feed their charges properly, and a semi-starved pony is a poor companion up a steep hill. These syces, being poorly paid, either steal the ponies' grain and sell it, or fail to buy sufficient, pocketing the proceeds. If the syce says he has no money to buy sufficient grain, the cost should be advanced to him, and deducted from the pony hire at the end of the tour.

Backs of animals should be examined daily for saddle sores, and if any are found, they should be treated at once. A supply of iodoform will be found useful for this purpose. All animals should be carefully inspected for saddle sores and girth galls before starting the tour, and any found suffering from these rejected. Shoes should be looked at occasionally, and loose or worn ones replaced.

Mules are invariably well looked after by their drivers, and the traveller need not worry about them.

Where a party is pressed for time, and double marches are being made, double rates must be paid, nor can double marches be made every day, especially with coolie transport. In the case of coolies, if the tour is a long one, a halt every eight days or so will be of benefit. Clothes can be washed, etc., and it may be mentioned here that Dhobies are available only in Kalimpong, Darjeeling, and Gantok. On the road, the bearer will wash out small articles, and a supply of soap should be taken for this purpose.

PRESENTS TO OFFICIALS AND MONASTERIES.

IN Tibet, when calling on a Tibetan of rank, it is the custom of the country that one should never go emptyhanded. Therefore should the traveller have occasion to visit a Tibetan notable, or a monastery, he should make suitable presents, These presents should always be accompained by a ceremonial silk scarf.

In the case of monasteries, a money present is most appreciated, and amounts varying from Rs. 5 in the case of a small institution, to Rs. 20 in that of a large monastery, will be found suitable.

The officials most likely to be met with in Tibet will be Depons, or Generals, and Jongpens, or District Magistrates, of the fourth and fifth rank respectively. For these suitable presents would consist of the following

1 Tin Biscuits.
1 Box Toilet Soap.
1 Small Bottle Scent

The whole to be accompanied by a silk ceremonial scarf, known as Kata.

A servant should be instructed to bring these gifts in on a tray, shortly after the traveller has seated himself with his host. who after glancing at them, will wave them away, when they should be handed over to one of the servants of the house.

For tours in Tibet which are arranged by the Himalayan Hotel, Kalimpong, Tibetan servants are sent, and these are well versed in Tibetan etiquette, and will put their employer wise as to what is the correct procedure on all occasions.

Cash presents to monasteries should be handed to the lama guide who has shewn the party round.

MAILS AND TELEGRAMS.

SHOULD the traveller desire his mails forwarded on while he is on tour, this can be arranged by leaving at his office a list of the Post and Telegraph Offices through which he passes, and the dates at which he will arrive at each.

To catch him, letters should be posted in Calcutta four days prior to the arrival of the addressee at any given post office. They should be addressed "care of the Postmaster, To Await Arrival." The name and address of the sender should be clearly written on the covers to facilitate return in the event of their being missed.

Telegrams reach any Telegraph Office in Sikkim or Tibet within a few hours of despatch from any place in Bengal. Undernoted are the Post and Telegraph Offices in Sikkim and Tibet.

Sikkim.	*Tibet.*
Rhenock.	Yatung.
Gnatong.	Pharijong.

Rungpo.
Gantok.

Gyantse.
(For this place letters should be posted six days ahead from Calcutta.)

MONEY.

IT is neither wise nor necessary to carry large sums of money on tours in Sikkim and Tibet.

Advances of pay and hire money for transport are paid either before or after the trip, and need not be carried. Dak Bungalow fees are payable in advance, so that only expenses for food, etc., on the road need be allowed for.

For a party of four, if Rs. 15 per day is allowed, this should be sufficient cash to carry for current expenses, and leave a small reserve for emergencies.

Cheques, if drawn on a Calcutta Bank, can sometimes be cashed in Kalimpong or Darjeeling, but the most convenient method, if it is desired to purchase curios or such like in Gantok, Yatung or Gyantse, is to purchase a hundi from a firm in Kalimpong which has branches in those places.

On frequented routes, and at Post Offices, notes are accepted and can be changed for cash.

Elsewhere all money must be carried in Rupees, with a fair proportion of small change. Indian money is current everywhere.

While the hill-peoples are honest, it is not wise to place temptation in their way by leaving money lying about in bungalows, etc., or in unlocked boxes.

TIPS.

TIPS will be expected by the servants and transport personnel of the tour. These may be given after the trip is over, provided the men have worked well, and given satisfaction, and may be of the following amounts.

Cook, bearer, sweeper, and coolies... One day's pay for each week's service.

Syces and muleteers............say Rs. 2/8/- for each week of the tour.

Tips to Chowkidars have been dealt with elsewhere.

CHITS.

AT the end of the tour the servants will require chits as to their conduct and capabilities, and these may be given, and, in the interest of future travellers, it is well that these should not be too laudatory.

THE TIFFIN BASKET.

WHEN a tiffin coolie is taken, he should be lightly loaded, or he will lag behind, and much inconvenience will be caused by his late arrival at the place fixed for lunch, or at the end of the march. Wherever camping tours are undertaken, such a man will be indispensable, as for these trips all crockery and cutlery, etc, must be carried by the tourist. The heavier and more bulky cooking pots can be carried along with the other heavy luggage, but the tiffin coolie should carry the wherewithal to make fresh tea, and so forth, immediately on arrival in the camping place. The heavy luggage may not arrive for some considerable time after the traveller. Suitable equipment for a tiffin basket for four people would be as follows:

1 Flat-bottomed kettle.
1 Small degchie, with detachable handle.
1 Primus, or other stove.
1 Flask Methylated spirit.
4 Enamelled plates.
4 Small enamelled bowls.
4 Enamelled mugs.
6 Knives.
2 Jharans.
6 Forks.
6 Dessert Spoons.
Pepper, salt, tea, sugar and butter receptacles.
1 Large Thermos.
1 Water bottle.
Hygienic cans for sandwiches, cut meats, etc.,
Tin opener and corkscrew.
Paper serviettes.

A good supply of matches.

The primus can be filled with kerosene and carried full.

COMPOSITION OF PARTIES.

THE ideal number for a tour party is four, and is best if composed of all one sex, or two couples. This is on account of certain bungalows possessing only two bedrooms, which means overcrowding if more than two persons have to occupy either, and also where only one room is available.

In the event of parties containing more than four people, at least one camp bed should be carried, as often not more than four beds are supplied, and it is uncomfortable for one of the party to have to sleep on a table, or in a deck chair.

MEDICINE CHEST.

IT is advisable to carry a few medicines on tour, as sickness can often be nipped in the bud by the use of a few simple remedies in its early stages. They will also be found useful in treating servants for small ailments. The following list may be useful as a basis for making up a small medicine chest.

Enos Fruit Salt.	Vaseline.
Castor Oil.	Iodoform.
Bisurated Magnesia.	Chlorodyne.
Iodine.	Germolene.

Aspirin.
Quinine.
Throat Pastilles.
Court Plaster.
Bandages.
Lint and Cotton Wool.
Scissors.
Needle and Thread.
Brandy.

LITERATURE.

ON tour, especially in the cold weather, when the evenings are long, the traveller will find that a few well chosen books will help to while away the hour or so intervening between dinner and bedtime.

In some of the bungalows a few books will be found, but as these are very old, and often mutilated, the tourist should take along a few of his own.

Apart from one or two favourite bedside books, the following are suggested, as dealing with Sikkim and Tibet, they will tell him something of the lands and the peoples he is among.

Lepcha Land......................F. Donaldson.
The Land of the Lama. D. Macdonald.
The People of Tibet...........Sir Charles Bell.
Sikkim and Bhutan. J. Claude White.

Any magazines not required after perusal may be left in the bungalows for the use of later travellers, and the fact of their donation noted in the Visitors' Book.

BOOTS.

COMFORTABLE footwear is essential. Sore and blistered feet will destroy all the pleasure of a trip, and every precaution should be taken to prevent this.

It is best if boots and shoes are well broken in before starting, either by soaking in oil, or by use, the latter being the best method. Riding boots are quite useless, as the tourist must walk over quite a lot of the road, and topboots, when walking downhill, give bad blisters on the heels.

Good heavy ammunition boots are the best for men, and stout ankle boots for women, and both may, if desired, be hobnailed. A pair of comfortable slippers is a great relief after the day's march is done, and should not be forgotten.

Woollen socks and stockings are the best, and should be thick. To avoid chafing, boric powder may be dusted inside them before putting them on, and the toes and heels rubbed on the outside with soap.

In the event of blisters developing, they should be pricked with a sterilised needle, Germoline applied, and a lint and cottonwool pad placed over them to protect them from further chafing while marching.

PESTS.

SIKKIM in th3 Rains is full of leeches, up to elevations of 10000 feet, and these make it impossible to get away from the beaten track. One dare not, moreover, sit down to rest, by the wayside, except on dry rock, as the leeches, wherever there is damp, rapidly close in and make things unpleasant.

On no account, once a leech has got a hold should it be violently pulled off, as a sore will result, which may turn septic, and give much trouble. The best way of removing them is to carry a small salt bag, a brief application of which will soon cause them to release their grip and drop off. If salt is not available, a good substitute is tobacco.

On arrival in the bungalow, iodine should be applied to the bites, and no alarm need be felt should they continue to ooze blood for even a considerable time.

There is no absolute protection against the leech obtaining a hold on the legs and body, but properly rolled putties, and boots with the tongues sewn into the uppers make it more difficult for the pest to reach the skin. The best protection is to avoid brushing against any foliage.

The leech is not found in Tibet.

Malarial mosquitoes are prevalent in the lower valleys of Sikkim during and just after the rains, and precautions in the form of mosquito nets are necessary. Quinine should be taken as a prophylactic. Tibet is fortunately free from all dangerous pests, but a kind of gnat found in the summer in the Chumbi Valley can be a nuisance. Beyond local irritation, however, which may be allayed by a face cream, no harm need be feared.

DANDIES AND CARRYING CHAIRS.

DANDIES for adults, and carrying chairs for children up to five years of age may be hired for touring purposes.

They are however, not recommended, as they are slow, uncomfortable, and very expensive, a dandy costing anything from twelve to fifteen rupees a day. It is not, moreover, advisable to take young children on tour as medical attention in the event of sickness is difficult to obtain.

MEDICAL ATTENDANCE.

MEDICAL attendance can be obtained in the undernoted places only, and in case of emergency, a doctor can as a rule be sent out to parties who are held up by accident or sickness, on information being sent in by runners.

DARJEELING	Hospitals and doctors.
KALIMPONG.	Several doctors (Men and Women) and hospital.
GANTOK.	Civil Surgeon and hospital.
PEDONG.	Sub-Assistant Surgeon and dispensary.
YATUNG.	Sub-Assistant Surgeon and hospital.
GYANTSE.	Military Surgeon and hospital.

MOUNTAIN SICKNESS.

MOUNTAIN sickness is liable to overtake some travellers, strong equally as much as weak, but it is very seldom experienced at heights below 12000 feet.

When it does occur, the symptoms are usually a dull heavy feeling, a headache, loss of appetite and sickness. A dose of aspirin and a rest will as a rule put the matter right.

In extreme cases, however, marked by severe pains in the head, continual sickness and depression, the only remedy is to descend to lower elevations, and this should be done at once.

Mountain sickness can to a great extent be avoided by not overdoing things in the matter of too long marches, climbing and so forth, until somewhat acclimatised to the rare atmosphere.

SIRDARS AND INTERPRETERS.

A knowledge of Hindustani or Nepalese will render the service of an interpreter unnecessary in Sikkim or the Darjeeling District, but parties who have no member speaking either of these tongues are recommended to take a Sirdar or interpreter who can speak English to deal with coolies, chowkidars, etc.

In Tibet, an interpreter is necessary, as without being able to get into touch with the Tibetans along the road a lot of the interest of a trip will be missed.

An interpreter, who will also supervise the muleteers and servants, will expect Rs. 5/- per day, and the expenses of his riding animal, another Rs. 4/- daily. He should speak English well, and also Tibetan, Hindustani and Nepalese.

Experienced men, speading, reading, and writing all the above languages, may be obtained through the Himalayan Hotel, Kalimpong, which guarantees their efficiency and knowledge of the country and people.

Except in the case of large parties taking a considerable number of coolies, a Sirdar is unnecessar as the supervision of the men can easily be done by a member of the party. A Sirdar's wages will be about Rs. 4/- per day.

GLARE GLASSES.

GLARE glasses should be taken on every trip, and should always be used when there is snow about in any large patches.

Snowblindness, while not particularly dangerous, is very painful, and may always be avoided by the use of antiglare glasses. The cure for snowblindness, if contracted, is simple. A few drops of castor oil in the eyes, which should be bandaged, will quickly afford relief.

The type of glasses recommended is that used by motorists, with complete protection from dust. No metal should touch the skin. This pattern is much to be preferred to the ordinary tinted spectacles, which allow the wind and dust to get in behind the lenses into the eyes.

COOLIES AND MULETEERS.

THE muleteers and coolies that the traveller in Sikkim and Tibet takes along with him are, though dirty, and, as a rule, especially when wet, odoriferous, an interesting crowd in themselves. Women as well as men carry loads, the former putting up as good a show as the latter. Muledrivers are invariably Tibetans, and one could not wish for more cheery and hard working servants.

The coolies may be drawn from several of the hill tribes but are as a rule Bhuteas, Sherpas, or Nepalis. Sherpas are considered the best, and provided the Everest Expeditions with their best men.

It is sometimes difficult to obtain coolies during the annual Kali Puja festival, when only the promise of extra pay will induce them to leave tha fleshpots of the bazaars. This applies, of course, to Hindus, but all the hill peoples make these Pujas an occasion for a holiday.

The Tibetan muleteers will take the road at any time.

PHOTOGRAPHY.

THE traveller will find endless subjects for his camera in Sikkim and Tibet, both human and scenic. The people do not object to being photographed, but the poorer classes will usually clamour for 'Bukshish' if they pose for a picture.

For Tibet, the writer has found that with ordinary standard Kodaks, in ordinary bright weather, an exposure of 1/25th seconds, with an aperture of about F8 or 9, on standard lenses, gives good results. A slightly larger stop may be used for Sikkim.

On cloudy days, of course, timing varies.

Films exposed in the hills are best developed in the hills, and this can be arranged for at either Kalimpong or Darjeeling, by professional photographers who undertake this kind of work.

For distant snow views, a telephoto lens is almost indispensable, if any thing more than a thin white line above the middle distance is required. Colour and sky filters also improve photographs.

BEGGARS.

BEGGARS will be met with all over the hills, usually Tibetans, with whom the profession is practically hereditary. The traveller must not think that the mendicant fraternity of Tibet are being rude when they protrude their tongues at him, it is merely a sign of respect and politeness from the lower orders of that country.

CAMPING EQUIPMENT.

UNLESS a camping tour is being made, or the route deviates from the main routes along which the dakbungalows are placed, it is not necessary for the tourist to carry anything in the way of cooking utensils, lamps, or furniture and crockery. He will find everything necessary in the well appointed bungalows.

For camping tours the following equipment is suggested:—

1 60 lb tent for each two persons.
1 camp cot per person.
1 camp dining table.
1 camp bath.
1 camp chair per person.
1 hurricane lantern per tent.
1 canvas bucket.
1 wash basin with cover per person.
1 ground sheet per tent.
1 pal for every six coolies.
1 pal for personal servants.
Stoves for camp cooking.

Camping requisites should be brought with the party. Except in the case of the Himalayan Hotel, it is not possible to hire these in the touring centres. Camping should be avoided during the rains, on account of pests.

A tiffin basket fitted for the number of persons in the party will be found convenient.

Cooking pots, etc., etc., sufficient for the party must, of course, be taken along.

FACE CREAMS AND TOILET PREPARATIONS.

FACE creams should be used with circumspection especially in Tibet. It will be found in many cases that the skin exposed to the sun and wind will crack and peel off, but on no account should face cream be applied to such chapped surfaces during the actual march. If this is done, the face will practically fry. Only when in the bungalows, after the march is over for the day, should lanoline, cold cream, or some such preparation be applied.

Before starting in the morning the remains of this cream should be carefully removed, and the skin liberally dusted with powder to get it perfectly dry.

Protection from the wind can be obtained by wearing a silk scarf across the lower part of the face, or by wearing a face mask, the latter being easily made in a few moments from an old handkerchief.

In Tibet, one frequently meets the Tibetans themselves wearing these masks, on which they paint grotesque features.

Bathing in Tibet and northern Sikkim should not be too freely indulged in, owing to the risk of chill. In Gyantse, as far as the garrison was concerned it used to be a medical order that rank and file should not bathe more than once a week.

ADVANCES OF PAY TO SERVANTS, Etc.

ADVANCES of pay and hire money of animals may, and indeed must, be given to the servants and mule hirers before starting out on the tour, the balance being paid after the return.

This arrangement, besides being the custom, is also convenient for the traveller, as it saves him from having to carry large sums of money. The following advances may be safely made.

To the mule and pony owners.	1/3rd of the total hire.
To coolies.	1/3rd of the pay they will earn.
To servants.	1/3rd of the pay they will earn.

The cook may also be given an advance of Rs. 10 wherewith to make bazaar purchases. Further amounts should not be given until he has rendered an account of the first advance.

It will be found as a general rule that tour servants are very honest, and advances may be given with perfect safety.

During a lifetime spent in the Eastern Himalayas, the writer has never heard of tour coolies or servants deliberately robbing their employers of goods or money. In cases where either has been lost it has been due to accident and not design.

EXTRA KIT FOR SERVANTS AND COOLIES.

FOR tours which take them to high elevations and in the rains and cold weather, extra kit may have to be provided for the staff, at the traveller's expense. This will be as below.

For the rains. An umbrella per man of the personal staff, and one bamboo ghoom, or one waterproof sheet per coolie.

For cold weather and high elevation tours. For each servant, a pair of warm socks, a pair of boots, and a thick blanket.

Mule drivers receive no extra kit at any time.

EXPENSES.

THE expense of a tour will of course vary considerably according to the degree of comfort and luxury desired by the party making it.

Average expenses will work out on lines similar to those given below, which have been worked out for a party of four on a ten day tour, Items are given per day, and are for mule transport, coolies will be slightly more expensive, as four coolies carry one mule load, in practice.

4 mules for personal baggage	@ Rs. 2/8......	Rs. 10-0-0
2 mules for stores...............	@ Rs. 2/8......	Rs. 5-0-0
4 riding mules	@ Rs. 3/8......	Rs. 14-0-0
1 Cook	@ Rs. 3	Rs. 3-0-0
1 Bearer...	@ Rs. 3	Rs. 3-0-0
1 Sweeper......	@ Rs. 1/8......	Rs. 1-8-0
1 Tiffin coolie	@ Rs. 1/4......	Rs. 1-4-0
Tip to bungalow chowkidar.		Rs. 1-0-0
Dak bungalow fees		Rs. 8-0-0
Messing averaging Rs. 20 per day		Rs. 20-0-0
Total per day.		Rs. 66-12-0
Cost per head per day.		Rs. 16-11-0

Total cost of tour for four persons for 10 days.
Rs. 665 approximately.

The above rate list does not include drinks, the cost of which will be extra, but they can probably be carried with the same transport.

Walking parties should do a 10 days' tour, everything included, for an all-in amount of Rs. 130 per head. It is, of course, quite possible to tour on very little, provided one is content to live on the country, and do one's own cooking. In such cases a couple of coolies would be sufficient, while food should not cost more than two or three rupees a day. If a small tent is carried, dak bungalow fees can also be saved.

HEART SUBJECTS.

THOSE suffering from weak or dilated hearts should on no account proceed on a tour in Sikkim or Tibet.

MAPS.

A VERY rough sketch map is given with this volume, but the tourist is recommended to obtain the maps of Sikkim, the Darjeeling District and Tibet, which are issued by the Government, Survey of India, and sold retail by the Map Record and Issue Office, 18, Wood Street. Calcutta. The following Sheets will be found most useful, and are on a scale of 4 miles to 1 inch.

Sheet No. 78A and 78D	Sikkim and Darjeeling.
Sheet No. 78E	Tibet.
Sheet No. 78C	Darjeeling and Jalpaiguri Districts

If larger scale maps are required these can be obtained from the same source.

The price of each sheet is Rs. 1/8/-. Postage extra.

CLIMBING.

ALL information regarding climbing in this part of the Himalayas may be obtained from the Hon. Secretary, Himalayan Climbing Club, Darjeeling, who will be able to advise as to the best times of the year, equipment, etc., etc.

BIBLIOGRAPHY.

The Land of the Lama	Macdonald.
The People of Tibet	Bell.
Tibet Past & Present.	Bell.
My Journey to Lhasa	David Neel (Madame)
Trans-Himalaya	Sven Hedin.
We Tibetans	Rinchen Lhamo.
Round Kinchenjunga	Freshfield.
To Everest through Tibet.	Noel.
Folk Stories from Tibet	Macdonald.
The Unveiling of Lhasa	Candler.
To Lhasa in Disguise	MacGovern.
Sikkim and Bhutan	Claude White.

SPECIMEN TOURS.

BELOW are given outline tours varying from a couple of days to several weeks duration. These tours can, of course, be modified, or linked up to make a longer trip. They can also be shortened by doing a double march occasionally in the one day. Days for halts are not included in these outlines.

In the specimen tours given the figures in between the stages denote the mileage.

TOURS WITH KALIMPONG AS A BASE.

2 days.

1. Kalimpong-12-Rississum-12-Kalimpong.

3 days.

2. Kalimpong-12-Rississum - 8 - Pasheting - 20-Mal (for Jalpaiguri.)

3. Kalimpong-13 - Pedong - 7 - Rississum - 12 - Kalimpong.

4. Kalimpong, by short cut-5-Melli-6-Tarkhola-by short cut-9-Kalimpong.

4 days.

5. Kalimpong-13-Pedong-5-Rhenock-12-Rississum-12-Kalimpong.

6. Kalimpong-14-Lopchu- 13 - Senchal (Tiger Hill)-18-Peshok-9-Kalimpong.

6 days.

7. Kalimpong-9-Peshok- 5 - Lopchu - 10 - Jorebungalow-4-Darjeeling-7½-Badamtam-18-Kalimpong.

7 days.

8. Kalimpong - 13 - Pedong - 14 - Pakyong - 11-Gantok-12-Bardang-12-Rangpo-11-Melli-5-Kalimpong.

8 days.

9· Kalimpong-17½-Badamtam-12½-Chakung-13-Rinchenpong -10 -Pemayangtse -10 -Rinchenpong -13 - Chakung-12½-Badamtam-17½-Kalimpnog.

11 days.

10. Kalimpong -13- Pedong -14- Pakyong -11-Gantok-10-Karponang -12-Changu -12-top of Nathu La and return to Changu-12-Karponang-10-Gantok-12-Bardang-17-Tar Khola-9-Kalimpong.

12 days.

11. Kalimpong-9-Peshok-15- Jorebungalow-8½-Jorepokri -10- Tonglu -14- Sandakphu -12½- Phalut-17-Dentam-11-Pemayangtse-10-Rinchenpong-13-Chakung -12½-Badamtam-17½-Kalimpong.

12. Kalimpong-13-Pedong-5-Rhenock -3-Ari-4-Rongli-9½-Sedonchen-9-Gnatong-5-Kupup-5 to top of Jelap La and back to Kupup-14-Sedonchen-13½-Ari-8-Pedong-13-Kalimpong.

13. Kalimpong-13-Pedong-8-Ari-13½-Sedonchen-2-Gnatong-10, through Kupup, visit Jelap La, and return to Kupup-8-Changu-12, visit Nathu La and return to Changu-12-Karponang-10- Gantok-12-Bardang-17-Tar Khola-9-Kalimpong.

14. Kalimpong-13-Pedong-8-Ari-13½-Sedonchen -14-Kupup-16-Yatung-14-Champithang-14-Changu-12-Karponang -10-Gantok -11- Pakyong -14- Pedong -13-Kalimpong.

16 days.

15. Kalimpong -14- Rungpo -12- Bardang -12-Gantok-13-Dikchu-11- Singhik -8-Toong-5- Chungtang-13-Lachen-13-Chungtang-5-Toong -8- Singhik-11- Dikchu-13-Gantok-11-Pakyong-14-Pedong-13-Kalimpong.

16. Kalimpong-13-Pedong-8-Ari-13½-Sedonchen -14-Kupup-16- Yatung-12- Gautsa-16- Pharijong-16-Gautsa- 12- Yatung -14- Champithang -14- Changu-12-Karponang -10-Gantok -12- Bardang -12- Rungpo -14-Kalimpong.

18 days.

17. Kalimpong -14- Rungpo -12- Bardang -12 Gantok-13-Dikchu-11- Singhik-8- Toong-5- Chungtang

-10-Lachung-8-Yumthang-8-Lachung-10-Chungtang-5-Toong-8-Singhik-11-Dikchu-13-Gantok-11-Pakyong-14-Pedong-13-Kalimpong.

20 days.

18. Kalimpong-17½- Badamtam-12½- Chakung-13-Rinchenpong-10-Pemayangtse-7-Tingling-7-Yoksun-5-Nibi-6-Bakyim-6-Jongri-6-Bakyim-6-Nibi-5- Yoksun-7-Tingling-7-Pemayangtse-11-Dentam-17- Phalut-12½-Sandakphu-14-Tonglu-10- Jorepokri-8½-Jorebungalow-15-Peshok-9-Kalimpong.

22 days.

19. Kalimpong -13- Pedong -14- Pakyong -11-Gantok-13-Dikchu-11-Singhik-8- Toong-5-Chungtang-13-Lachen-13-Thangu-10-Giagong-13-Chu Lhamo-3 to Donkya La ,and 3-Mome Samdong-10-Yumthang-8-Lachung-10-Chungtang-5- Toong-8-Singhik-11-Dikchu-13-Gantok-12-Bardang-12-Rungpo-14-Kalimpong.

25 days.

20. Kalimpong-17½-Badamtam-12½- Chakuug-13 Rinchenpong-10-Pemayangtse-7-Tingling-7-Yoksun-5-Nibi-6- Bakyim -6- Jongri -9- Alukthang -9- foot of Guicha La-visit Pass and return to camp-9-Alukthang-9-Jongri-10-Churung-12- Gamothang-13- Miguthang-15-Nayathang-12- Phalut-12½- Sandakphu-14-Tonglu-10- Jorepokri-8½- Jorebungalow-15- Peshok-9- Kalimpong.

30 days.

21. Kalimpong -13- Pedong-8- Ari-13-½Sedonchen-14-Kupup-16-Yatung-12-Gautsa-16-Pharijong-21-Tuna-12-Dochen-12-Kala-14-Samoda-14-Kangma-14½-Saugong-14½-Gyantse-14½-Saugong-14½-Kangma-14-Samoda-14-Kala-12-Dochen-12-Tuna-21-Pharijong-16-Gautsa-12- Yatung -14- Champithang -14- Changu -12-Karponang -10- Gantok-12- Bardang -12- Rungpo -14-Kalimpong.

TOURS WITH DARJEELING AS A BASE.

ALL tours as given from Kalimpong as a starting point may be linked up with Darjeeling. For instance Darjeeling is 4 miles from Jorebungalow, and tours passing through this place can also be started from Darjeeling.

Darjeeling to Gantok may be done in 3 days confortably, via Peshok, Tarkhola, Rangpo, and Bardang, or Badamtam, Sankakhola, and Bardang, and thus the traveller gets on the routes to northern Sikkim and the Pass country, and if he crosses to Kalimpong, he is at once on the Trade Route to Tibet.

* * * *

On tours Nos. 18, 19, 20, tents must be taken for several of the camps, nor are riding animals able to be taken all the road. Details of transport arrangements will be found in the descriptions of the tours given later in the book.

FISHING AND SHOOTING CENTRES.

THE following centres in the Teesta Valley are considered to afford excellent fishing, the most important fish being the mahseer, which in this river attains a considerable size. Fish weighing up to 35 lbs are fairly common. There are comfortable and convenient bungalows all along the river.

Sevoke.	Forest bungalow.
Kalijhora.	P. W. D. Bungalow.
Riyang.	D. H. Ry. Bungalow.
Teesta Bridge.	P. W. D. Bungalow.
Melli.	P. W. D. Bungalow.
Rangpo.	Dak Bungalow.

Game is plentiful round Sevoke, and this is the best centre for shooting parties. Tents should be taken for accommodation. All game, from elephants downwards are likely to be met with, so that suitable weapons should be taken. Beaters may be obtained locally. Unless a proclaimed rogue, however the shooting of elephant is prohibited.

All information regarding shooting and fishing in the Darjeeling District may be obtained from the Honorary Secretary, Darjeeling Shooting and Fishing Club, Kurseong, D. H. Ry. Membership of this Club, without which permission to shoot and fish will not be granted, costs Rs. 10/-. An extra fee of Rs. 10/- each will be levied for shooting and fishing permits. This club leases all the available shooting preserves and rivers in the Darjeeling District.

The Sikkim Game Laws are given in Appendix No 2 of this volume, and all details will be found therein.

KALIMPONG.

KALIMPONG, 4300 feet above sea-level, is situated on the Deolo-Rinkingpong Ridge, above the east bank of the Teesta River. It lies due east of Darjeeling, 28 miles by road from that town, and is the headquarter station of the Kalimpong sub-division of the Darjeeling District of Bengal.

It is within 14 hours of Calcutta, by rail and car, the journey to Siliguri being made in the Eastern Bengal State Railway mail train, and from thence, by car through the Terai belt and along the beautiful Teesta Valley, arrival in Kalimpong being made in time for a late breakfast. If the Darjeeling Himalayan train is taken from Siliguri to Kalimpong Road, the visitor arrives in Kalimpong a few hours later, the latter station being 12 miles by road from Kalimpong. This last 12 miles is done by car.

Kalimpong is served by excellent approach roads, and also has first class motor roads within its limits. It is well served by taxis, the average rates of hire between Siliguri and Kalimpong and Siliguri and Kalimpong Road Station being Rs. 25 and Rs. 10 respectively.

The climate is mild, the maximum temperature seldom exceeding 75 degrees Fahrenheit, the minimum never dropping below 34 degrees. The temperature runs 10 degrees warmer than Darjeeling all the year round. The rainfall also is moderate, averaging 80 inches per year, nor does Kalimpong get the heavy mists to anything like the extent of Darjeeling.

For these climatic reasons, many people find Kalimpong more suitable than hill stations of higher elevation, as a sanitarium, and children especially thrive in the place. Kalimpong is not unsuitable for heart subjects, and is yearly becoming more popular among the medical profession as a place to which to send convalescents from malaria and other fevers for recuperation.

The water supply is excellent. Water is collected in a reservoir at the headwaters of the Rilli River, some 13 miles away in the hills, and from there is piped in to subsidiary reservoirs, from which, after chlorination, it is distributed to consumers. Kalimpong has never experienced any epidemic of water-borne disease, nor do visitors suffer from that distressing complaint hill-diarrhœa.

Medical attention of the highest order is available in Kalimpong, at the Charteris Hospital, one of the largest in Bengal, outside of Calcutta.

This institution, run by the Scots Mission, has both men and lady doctors, and a highly efficient nursing staff, and in addition to the usual public wards, has one wing set aside for European patients, each of whom has his or her own private room.

Nowadays, visitors may obtain comfortable accommodation at the Himalayan Hotel, the most central building in the Station. Paying guests are received by several private families.

Those interested in agriculture and market gardening may spend an interesting morning inspecting the Government Demonstration Farm, situated below the Bazar. Here experimental work is carried on with the object of improving the crops of the district, and good tested seeds are distributed among the cultivators.

Kalimpong is the centre of the eastern and central Tibet wool trade, and in the winter the town is full of Tibetan traders and their muleteers. In the Tibetan quarters at the northern end of the bazaar the photographer will find many interesting subjects for his camera. The cold weather is Kalimpong's busiest time, as the wool must be brought in then, during the rains the wool packs get wet and heavy, and damp is bad for the wool. In the hot weather the Tibetans will not come to India.

During the first week of December, the annual Kalimpong Mela, or Fair, is held. At this the local people, and those of the neighbouring Native States of Bhutan and Sikkim, exhibit their produce, for the best specimens of which good prizes in cash are offered. The local European population makes this the occasion of a European week, which is attended by many of the local tea planters from the Dooars and the Darjeeling tea gardens. Sports, gymkhanas, concerts, and dances, help to while away the time.

From one end of Kalimpong to the other is not far short of 4 miles. At the northern end are the well known St. Andrew's Colonial Homes, a philanthropic institution founded by Dr. J. A. Graham, and the late Mrs. Graham. Here nearly 700 Anglo-Indian children are brought up and started in the world, the enterprise being almost entirely supported by public charity. A staff of over 70 is employed at these Homes. Visitors are cordially welcomed, and a most interesting day may be spent in seeing the varied activities that go on. The children are domiciled in cottages, 30 or so in each, each house being under the charge of a 'House Mother' and 'House Auntie.' One sees children of all ages ranging from babies in arms to young men and women of eighteen or nineteen years of age. The Homes are located on the eastern slopes of Deolo Hill.

At the foot of Deolo, below the Tibetan Monastery, a new-looking place, but worth a visit, is the Scots Mission Compound. Here will be seen the Boys' and Girls' High Schools, the Charteris Hospital, the various Mission-houses, and the Kalimpong Mission Industries. At the last the local people are taught and employed in various arts and crafts, such as carpentry, leather work, carpet making, and embroidery. These Industries are also well worth a visit.

Standing out against the hillside, the weathered pile of the Macfarlane Memorial Church, with its belfry, affords a landmark for miles around, and is the first object that strikes the eye when approaching Kalimpong from the Plains. The house of Dr. J. A. Graham, D. D. C. I. E. the 'Father of Kalimpong,' is situated immediately below this church. To this gentleman is entirely due the development of Kalimpong, as it was due to his advice and to his energy, that Government decided to open the place as a hill-station.

The Bazaar lies along and below the saddle connecting the hills of Deolo and Rinkingpong. In the main street will be found good general shops, run by Indians, at which almost everything necessary for the visitor and the tourist can be purchased. Prices are about one anna in the rupee dearer than Calcutta. Saturdays and Wednesdays are the big bazaar days, when the people flock in from the countryside to sell their produce and to make their purchases of the necessaries they cannot grow themselves. On these days the bazaar is a kaleidoscope of moving colours, for the women especially on their brightest saries and shawls for these occasions. Kalimpong is possibly the most cosmopolitan of hill stations in the Himalayas. Here one meets Tibetans, Mongolians, Chinese, Burmese, Nepalis, Lepchas, Bhutanese Marwaries, Ladakis, Bengalis, Punjabis, Kabulis, and Europeans, and every shade between.

There are few curio shops, but interesting souvenirs and sometimes really good pieces can be picked up in the Junk shops run by Chinese and Tibetans. The author has, for those really interested in Tibetan and Chinese art, a collection which will repay the time spent in examining the same. He is also prepared to dispose of duplicate pieces.

Next the Bazaar, at the foot of Rinkingpong Hill, are the Police Station, the Post and Telegraph Office, the Town Hall, and the Kutcherry and Treasury. There is no recognised Bank in Kalimpong, but the Himalayan Hotel will cash approved cheques on payment of the usual commission. These cheques must be on Calcutta Banks. The Dak-Bungalow is situated near the Kutcherry on the main motor road to Rinkingpong. On the approach road, at the 8th mile, will be seen the St. Joseph's Convent Girls' School, maintained by a French Order of nuns from Chandernagore. Small boys are also taken here. Both boarders and day scholars are accepted.

On the slopes of Rinkingpong will be seen numerous private residences, whose number is increasing yearly, especially now that certain stringent building restrictions have been removed. Rinkingpong can never become congested, as Darjeeling, as Government forbids the erection of more than one residence in each plot, which is roughly at least an acre in extent.

From Durpindara, the top of Rinkingpong Hill, formerly used as an artillery observation post, a wonderful view of the Teesta River, four thousand feet sheer below, is obtained, as well as, on a clear morning, a panorama of the snows, second only to that seen from Tiger Hill, near Darjeeling.

DETAILED TOURS.

FOR descriptive purposes three main tours have been selected, and these will take the tourist over almost every path, and to almost every bungalow of importance and interest. The three tours are the following:—

1. Kalimpong to Gyantse.
2. Kalimpong to the Donkya Pass.
3. Kalimpong to the Guicha Pass.

TOUR No. 1.

KALIMPONG to Gyantse, via Pedong, the Jelap La, and Phari Jong, returning via the Nathu La, and Gantok.

When leaving Kalimpong Bazaar, two roads offer for the traveller to Tibet, one, the lower and main trade route, the other, the shorter and upper road through the St. Andrew's Colonial Homes. As both these roads join a few miles from Kalimpong, and the upper will have been covered during visits to the Homes, the lower should be selected for the first day's march. On this lower road will be met the mule teams coming in from Tibet with wool and other merchandise, and some interesting subjects for the camera may offer.

2 Miles from the Kalimpong Bazaar, the Murray Road will be noticed going up to the left of the road, but this should not be taken. Just beyond where this road goes off, and past the wool godowns will be seen the Bhutan Darbar House, the residence of the popular young Bhutanese Minister, Raja S. T. Dorje, who spends several months every year in Kalimpong.

In this house are preserved as he left them, the rooms occupied by the Dalai Lama of Tibet, for several weeks, during his exile from his country in 1909-12. Priveleged persons are sometimes invited to inspect these apartments, but they are not open to the general public.

It may here be noted, that, as far as the Jelap pass, the mileage on the main trade route is counted from Teesta Bridge, so that the figures on the mileposts will show 10 miles more than the traveller has actually covered.

From the Bhutan Durbar House, the road ascends gradually to the 17 mile, practically shadeless all the way, and here the upper road, already mentioned, comes in on the left, at a small tea-house. A stiff climb of 1½ miles from this place, over a cobbled causeway brings the traveller to the village of Algarah, a recognised halting place for the mule teams. Here the road taken by the tourist turns off to the right, and is flagged by a sign post to Rississum, Labah and Dam-Dim.

2½ miles through magnificent forest, along a fine metalled level road, brings the traveller to the foot of the hill on the very top of which the Rississum Bungalow is perched. At the 2nd mile from Algarah, the path to Pedong, which will be taken the next morning, may be descried coming in on the left. The last ½ mile to the bungalow is a very stiff climb, also through virgin forest.

From the Rississum Bungalow, a wonderful panorama of the snows, across the whole of Sikkim is to be seen. Darjeeling and Kalimpong also stand out in the middle and near distances.

This bungalow is comfortable, but the water supply is very scanty. Water has to be brougnt from a distance of over one mile, from the head-waters of the Rilli. Baths should therefore be postponed till the next halt. At one time this resthouse had the reputation of being haunted, but on the many occasions on which the writer and his friends have stayed there no spiritual manifestations have occurred, nor has it been possible to obtain information of any snch.

The name Rississum, or properly, Rhi Ki Sum, means the "hill with three corners."

Descending the hill from Rississum, the Pedong path, noticed the day before running to the right at the 2nd milepost from Algarah, should be taken. From the point, a more or less gradual descent of about four miles brings the traveller to the main trade route once more, at the 19th milepost. On the way the monastery of Chu-Milk-Chan, the "Spring of Water" is passed. Pedong is reached after another three miles descent through cultivated land, the Dak-Bungalow being situated at the corner of a very well kept camping ground. Pedong bungalow is one of the most comfortable on the road.

The bazaar lies about ¾ mile beyond the bungalow, and here, in front of the Post Office, may be seen the Po or Incense Tree from which the place takes its name. Pedong is the headquarters of a large Roman Catholic Mission, a branch of the well-known French Mission Etrangeres, controlled at one time by the famous Father Desgodins. The present head is the Rev. Monsignor Jules Douenel. S. J., Prefect Apostolic of this part of the Himalayas. Monsignor Douenel always welcomes visitors, and an interesting hour may be spent looking over the various activities of the Mission.

Away on a spur across the Rishi Valley will be seen the outstation of this Mission called Maria Busti, while more to the north, opposite Pedong, will be descried the dak bungalows of Rhenock and Ari, and on a clear day, Sedonchen.

Before leaving Pedong, the next day, Frontier Passes will have to be shown to the Police, and one copy handed over to them. After this formality has been observed, the traveller will drop steeply down a zigzaging road for four miles to the Rishi Bridge, which marks the actual frontier between Sikkim and British India. Thence a steep climb of just over a mile brings him to the Sikkim Frontier Station of Rhenock. Here Passes will again have to be shown to the Sikkim Police, but should not be given up, each visitor signing his name in the register kept for the purpose.

Before leaving Rhenock, a visit should be paid by those interested in horticulture and fruit growing to the Chandra Nursery, where Rai Sahib Pradhan and his brother have a wondertul show of Sikkim orchids, flowering shrubs, and fruit trees.

Just across the pass, immediately below which Ari is situated, is the camping ground used by the muleteams, which was formerly a commissariat depot during the various Expeditions in this part of the country.

From Ari the road winds down for 4 miles through forest to Rongli, 'The Lepcha's Hut', where a halt may be made for lunch. Rongli, being only 2500 feet above sea level, is not suitable for a night's halt except in the winter. From Rongli to Gnatong, a distance by road of 18 miles, the road rises 10000 feet in elevation, most of this being accomplished in the 9 miles between Lingtam and Lingtu.

Crossing the Rongli Chu by an iron bridge, the road turns sharply to the right, and after passing through the village of Rongli, some ½ mile farther on, follows up the valley of the Rongli Chu, the scenery becoming grander every mile that is covered. At the 39th mile is the large posting station of Lingtam, a recognised halting place for the muleteams. From here a veritable staircase of cobbles, set in a causeway, leads the traveller up to Sedonchen, through forest, where a halt will be made for the night. Sedonchen, the 'Place of the great Se tree', is a lonely bungalow, not too comfortàble, but with wonderful views back over the road already covered. Darjeeling can be descried on its ridge away to the south.

The traveller is strongly advised to ride all the way between Lingtam and Lingtu, as the exertion of climbing may bring on mountain sickness in those unacclimatised to the heights. Sedonchen is 9500 feet above sea level.

Looking upwards from this bungalow, the heights of Lingtu will be seen towering some 4000 feet above, and over these the traveller must pass the next day.

The climb to Lingtu begins immediately on leaving the bungalow, and continues steadily for five miles, passing through the muleteams' halting place of Jeluk, where there are teashops and serais. Lingtu is marked by a few dak runners' huts, at one of which the traveller may obtain a good cup of tea, as the wife of one of the men runs a small teashop.

These dak runners have a very hard life. At the lower elevations the men run five miles at a stretch, but above Lingtu, this distance is reduced to 2½ miles, and this is more than enough, especially when the snow is down and a blizzard blowing. Whatever the weather, the dak goes through somehow, and many men have been lost and more injured through frostbite owing to their efforts to get through with their mails. In the entire twenty years the writer has spent in those parts the mail has only been held up some six times. Letters, carried day and night, reach Yatung 36 hours after being despatched from Kalimpong.

Near Lingtu are the ruins of a Tibetan fort, erected in 1887, in an attempt on the part of the Tibetan Government to occupy Sikkim. They were ejected with considerable loss by the Sikkim Expedition of 1888.

From Lingtu, two roads are available, each on a different side of the hill. The upper should be taken, as the lower is usually breached and ponies cannot get across. In the winter, the lower road is impassable owing to snow. At the 50th milepost a wonderful view of Kinchenjunga is to be had to the west, while to the east the panorama of the Plains of India lies spread out in the distance. From this spot a ride of 1¾ miles brings the traveller to the village of Gnatong, situated in a marshy hollow in the hills. In the winter, when the snow is down, care should be exercised on this part of the road, as the track is only a few inches wide, and when riding a nasty fall may result from the animal putting its foot into a hole.

Just before entering the village, the cemetery in which the casualties of the 1888 and 1904 Expeditions are buried, will be noticed on the left, marked by a cairn.

The Gnatong bungalow, though substantial, is cold, and big fires should be kept going. The chowkidar here is, at the time of writing, the best on the road, and is a very willing helper is cases of sickness due to height, or other cause.

Leaving Gnatong the next morning, the traveller drops down a ½ mile or so to where a small bridge spans a stream, and from thence climbs steadily up to the Tuko La, beyond which lie the rolling uplands known as the "Derby Downs" after the Derbyshire Regiment which operated here in 1888 and ejected the Tibetan levies. When the snow is about the Tuka La can be dangerous, owing to drifts, and care should be exercised at such times. A mile from Kupup, and three miles from Gnatong, the Nim La is crossed, after which the path drops steadily to the Kupup Bungalow, situated at the end of the Bidang Lake, the source of the Jaldakha River of the Bengal Dooars. This is a very fine example of a glacial lake, and is about ½ mile long.

Kupup, with only two rooms, was originally built as an emergency bungalow for travellers caught between the Jelap and Tuko Passes in bad weather, when to go forward or back was impossible. In winter, it is sometimes completely buried in snow, and is only found with some difficulty.

In May and June, the rhododendrons, from Sedonchen upwards are a sight to be remembered.

From Kupup a track goes across the mountains connecting with the Gantok-Nathu La road, meeting the latter a little above Changu.

3 Miles takes the traveller to the top of the Jelap Pass, the first mile or so following up the side of the Kupup Valley, but after this becoming a steep causeway zig-zagging up to the Pass.

The scenery is wild and magnificent, the jumble of peaks forming northern Sikkim being well defined.

The usual cairns and prayer-flags mark the actual summit of the Pass, from which a steep decent of ½ mile leads to a small lake. Chomolhari is visible on a clear day from this Pass, a small triangle of white on the northern horizon. A further descent of a couple of miles over the worst road in the world brings the traveller to the village of Langram, a poor collection of huts grouped round an old Chinese posting house, now more or less in disrepair. Only in the greatest emergency should a halt be made here.

Five miles below Langram, the path descending steeply the whole way through pine and rhododendron forest, is the abandoned settlement of Old Yatung, the former Chinese Frontier Observation and Customs Post. Here may be seen the old yamens of the Chinese officials, as well as the house accupied for some years by the woman missionary trader, Annie Taylor. A wall has been built across the valley, through the only gateway of which the road passes. It does not seem difficult, however, for an unauthorised traveller to have circumvented this by clambering along the mountain side above the end of the wall.

Still descending, and crossing and re-crossing the river, another three miles brings the tourist to Rinchengong, a large village in the Chumbi valley proper. Rinchengong is situated on the Amo Chu, and has many fine double storeyed houses, the property of wealthy wool traders. Passing through the narrow main lane of this settlement, the road then follows the left bank of the Amo Chu for a couple of miles, through Phema village, where the road to the Nathu La takes off, to Pibithang, the official residence of the Tibetan Trade Agent, the governor of the Chumbi valley.

Still another two miles march brings one to Yatung, the treaty Trade Mart, where a British Trade Agent has his headquarters, and a military escort.

The Dak bungalow is on the opposite bank of the river from the Trade Agency and the barracks, and is reached by a long wooden bridge. This bungalow is very comfortably furnished, and delightfully situated.

While in Yatung a call should be paid on the British Trade Agent, if he is in residence. He will always be glad to welcome visitors, as his is a lonely life, and fresh faces are always appreciated. The Chumbi Valley is delightful, and if a day is spent here, it will be profitably employed in exploring some of the nearby country, care of course being taken not to contravene the terms of the Tibet Pass.

The march to Gautsa, the next halting place, begins with a gradual ascent through a cultivated valley, with many prosperous villages and temples, until the Lingmathang Plain is reached. This is a broad expanse of greensward, with the river meandering through. It would be an ideal spot for a sanitarium, should one ever be opened in Tibet. Overlooking the plain is the Donka Monastery, which is worth visiting. The time can be spared, as the march is a short one.

From Lingmathang, the road climbs more steeply, through wild and magnificent scenery, crossing and re-crossing the river, which is now a torrent, dozens of times. Gautsa, 'the meadow of joy', is placed near the river bank, in a clearing, just above the Tibetan Mint, which should also be visited.

Gautsa is not too good a bungalow, but if large fires are kept up, is tolerable. It has only two rooms.

The road followed next day is one of the worst possible, boulder strewn, and steep in many places. Three miles climb from Gautsa brings the traveller to the Dotha Plain, a basin in the hills a mile long but narrow. Dotha has a wonderful water fall, which when frozen solid in the winter, is a magnificent sight. The only houses on this plain are the mail runners' huts, one of which is also a tea-shop. The trees now end, above Dotha only scanty stunted herbage is seen. The road follows the river on for another two miles, the path being a ledge cut in the hillside above the ravine.

Seven miles from Gautsa, the river is crossed for the last time, and the track crosses rolling downs for a couple of miles to the hamlet of Kamparab. From here to Pharijong, a distance of seven miles, the going is easy, the fort at Phari being visible while some four miles away. Behind the village rises the magnificent pile of Chomolhari.

Phari Jong is situated in the centre of a plain that bears the title of the 'Thang Pun Sum' 'The Plain of the Three Brothers'. Its name means 'The Hill made Glorious', a complete misnomer. Whatever Phari may have been in the past, at present it is the filthiest town in the world. Built originally on a low hill, the place is literally buried in its own filth. The bazaar and the Fort should be visited, if only to realise the squalor in which some people can live.

The Dak bungalow is not too comfortable, and fuel is a problem. Wood can be bought at a price, otherwise dried yak dung must be used. After leaving Phari, the latter is the only fuel available until Gyantse is reached.

Phari is not a place to linger in, and the next day's march of twenty one miles to Tuna should be begun early. The hamlet of Chukya, with its monastery, is passed four miles out across the plain, and from thence a gradual pull up of another four miles brings the traveller to the top of the Tang La, the true Himalayan watershed, (15,600 feet). The top is marked by the usual cairns and prayer flags.

A short steep drop of a ¼ mile ends at Shobra Shubra, the 'Whispering Waters', where there is a mail runners' hut. From Phari the mail is carried to Gyantse by mules, which trot along, covering the distance of 102 miles in two days. The animals are changed at each dak-bungalow, which is provided with stables and muledrivers for reliefs.

Tuna can be easily descried from the Tangla. and seems but a few miles off. It will be found, however, that the extreme clarity of the atmosphere at these heights is deceptive, It will take three full hours at least to reach the bungalow. The track lies across a gravel plain, and follows the telegraph line all the way. Tuna was used for several months as the headquarters of the Younghusband Mission in 1903-4, but is merely a collection of poor houses, with the dak bungalow a short distance from the village.

From Tuna to Saugong all the bungalows are of the same pattern, two rooms and bathrooms, with offices, enclosed in a walled compound, for shelter from the wind. That they were also built with an eye to defence is obvious. They are as comfortable as it is possible to make them, but fires are necessary all the time they are in occupation.

Most travellers will ask 'where is the Plateau, the tableland', that we learned about at school ? This flat tableland does not exist. The 'Plateau' consists of a series of old lake beds bounded by low weathered hills, except of course, where Chomolhari and other snow peaks border them.

Tuna is the coldest bnngalow on the road, and it will be left without regret. The next day's march is easy, 12 miles, to Dochen, on the bank of the great Hram Lake, the breeding ground of countless thousands of wildfowl. On the way, six miles from Tuna, will be noticed a small stream welling out from the cliff. This marks the place where there was a skirmish during the Mission of 1904, resulting in heavy Tibetan casualties. This place is called Guru. No habitations are to be seen except the villages near the bungalows, and possibly one or two black tents of the nomad shepherds and yak herds. Kyang and gazelle are frequently met with all along the road.

Dochen is a fairly comfortable place, sheltered from much of the wind that blows straight off the glaciers of Chomolhari across the Tuna plain. Besides the dak bungalow, there are only a few hovels, in which a couple of families of poverty stricken shepherds live. These can be seen milking their sheep every afternoon. It is advisable to use tinned milk at this stage.

The next day's trek follows the bank of the Hram Lake for six miles, to where its waters debouch through a gorge to join those of the Kala Lake, four miles away. This stream is crossed by a bridge, and is followed for four miles to the hamlet of Tsalu. Many ruins are scattered about this valley, and it is of interest to note that these were in the same condition over a hundred years ago, when the traveller Bogle passed this way. He was told, and the people still tell the same story, that these houses and villages were destroyed by Bhutanese raiders. Similar ruined houses are to be seen all along the road between Tuna and Gyantse, and the above reason for their abandonment is always given.

Kala dak bungalow, at the 56th milestone from Gyantse, and 12 miles from Dochen, is also out on a plain. Kala is noted for its dried fish, and every house in the village, some distance away on the edge of the lake contains a large stock of these, which are sent into Gyantse and Phari for sale or exchange for other necessaries. These fish are, however, very bony, and rather insipid to eat.

When the milestones were first erected on the Phari-Gyantse road, the local people invariably destroyed them, alleging that they were gods put up by the British to destroy their faith. Only after many years did this belief die out, and even at the present time some of these cairns can be seen scattered over the plain.

The Kala Valley is followed for 8 miles, to the east when the road turns north again. Once the Kala Valley is left, the whole scenery alters. Up to this point villages have been few, and the country very sparsely inhabited. Once the Kala Valley is left however, cultivation becomes general, villages are more numerous, and the whole valley of the Nyang Chu which is followed right to Gyantse, is a smiling countryside.

A march of four miles along the Nyang River brings the traveller to Samoda, the next halting place. Samoda is a large village, and fresh mutton and eggs can sometimes be purchased there.

From Samoda, the march of 14 miles through the Nyang Valley, past villages and monasteries, nestling up the side valleys, will be found easy. Kangma is the name of this halting place, and from here a cross track runs to Nagartse, on the Gyantse-

Lhasa road. This cross track saves several days for travellers from Phari to Lhasa.

A half mile beyond the Kangma bungalow is a hot spring close by the side of the road, while three miles farther on, the wonderful Red Idol Gorge is entered. It passes comprehension that the Tibetans allowed British troops to pass through this without offering resistance. Here a few determined men could hold up an army corps.

After mile through the gorge, the valley opens out again, and Saugong is reached after a total march of 14 miles from Kangma.

Only 14 miles now remain to be done to reach Gyantse, and as the road is easy, four hours should see the traveller comfortably ensconced in the Gyantse dak bungalow. From four miles distant from the city, the Tibetan Fort, perched on a high spur, is sighted, the town nestling at its foot. The Nyang is crossed by a bridge near the Jong, and turning sharp to the right after having crossed this, a ride of a ¼ mile brings one to the bungalow.

Gyantse is the third largest city in Tibet, and has a population of some seven thousand, including the lamas in the Palkhor Choide, the great monastery. The points of interest are the British Trade Agency, housed, with its military escort and followers, in a square fort to the south of the dak-bungalow, the Tibetan Fort, the Monastery, and the city itself. A call should be paid on the British post as soon after arrival as possible, and the officers stationed there will be pleased to suggest what sights should be seen, and the best way to see them.

At least three days should be spent in Gyantse, if a shorter halt is made, several interesting things will be missed.

The return journey as far as Yatung is made by the same route.

Leaving Yatung, the Amo Chu is followed as far as the village of Phema, where a track will be seen going off to the right, climbing steeply immediately after leaving the road. The road surface after a few miles, is execrable, being largely corduroy which has become displaced. In the rains this can be very unpleasant. The Kargyu Monastery, five miles above the Chumbi Valley is worth a visit.

Seven miles above this place is the bungalow of Champithang, where a halt will be made. On the road from the Monastery to the bungalow, wonderful views of the path from the Jelap to Rinchengong are obtained, as well as of the Pass country itself.

From Champithang to the top of the Nathu La takes about an hour. At every turn of this part of the road, fresh snow views are seen, including the wonderful mass of Chomolhari. It is six miles from the Nathu La to Changu bungalow, through Sharabthang, an old camping ground, and past several dark and gloomy tarns. The scenery is wild in the extreme, and of surpassing grandeur.

Changu Bungalow is situated at the end of the lake of the same name, in a basin surrounded by mountains. The Changu lake is beautiful, especially in the sun, and there was at one time a scheme to harness the waters falling from the lake, and instituting a big hydro-electric plant, to supply northern Bengal with power. At present the plan has been dropped, at any rate for the time being.

The road between Changu and Karponang is in places merely a ledge hewn out of the rock face of the gigantic cliffs, hundreds of feet above the brawling torrent. Some parts of the road are badly washed away in the rains, while in the winter this path is entirely closed after heavy snow. Near Karponang, the next halt, are several pretty waterfalls.

Karponang is a very fine new bungalow, and here the traveller will be very comfortable. The road from here to Gantok gradually descends through forest for five miles, after which it becomes a cart road and so continues on to Gantok, with fields and villages on either side. The road comes out immediately below the Gantok dak bungalow.

Gantok, the capital of Sikkim, is not an impressive town, and is at present painfully in the making. It is very scattered, from the British Residency at one end to the Palace at the other. The bazaar lies below the ridge on which the latter is placed. The town, if it can so be called, is lit by electricity. There is a High School, named after the present Maharaja Sir Tashi Namgyal, supervised by a British Head Master, and a Mission Girls' School, supervised by the Hon. Miss Mary Scott, a devoted missionary who has laboured for many years among the people of Sikkim.

If time is a consideration, the traveller may motor, in the dry weather, from Gantok to Siliguri or Kalimpong in the one day. If he decides to continue his trek however, he drops to a point on the Gantok-Rungpo Road, some three miles below the former place.

Here the path to Pakyong will be seen branching off to the left, the descent continuing to the Roro River, which is crossed at the village of Suram Se. A mile further on another river, the Takcham, is crossed, and the Rongni yet another mile on. From here the road climbs to the 4th mile from the Gantok road, where a mani wall and some graves are to be seen in a clearing in the forest. Another 4 miles brings the traveller to the resthouse of Pakyong. Looking back one can see Gantok defined on its ridge. Nearby is the Kartok Monastery, well worth a visit.

The next day's march takes the traveller to Rhenock. Leaving the Pakyong dak bungalow the path drops steadily for 5½ miles to where the Roro Chu runs into the Rungpo River. Crossing the former, the right bank of the Rungpo is followed to the Rorothang Bridge, which should be crossed. Here a signpost indicates the path to Rhenock, which is reached after a steep climb of 1¾ miles and a level track of another mile and a half.

From Rhenock the same road as that taken on the outward journey is taken to Kalimpong, with the exception that instead of turning off to Rississum at the 19th milepost, the Kalimpong Road is followed through Algarah direct. The march from Rhenock should be easily done in the one day.

TOUR No. 2.

KALIMPONG to the Donkya Pass, via Pakyong and Gantok, returning via Gantok and Rungpo.

The route as far as Gantok has already been described in detailed Tour No. 1.

From Gantok, a steady climb of nearly four miles is made to the Penlong Pass. From this, a descent of another four miles brings the traveller to a road junction, that to the right, which should not be taken, leading to Tumlong Jong, the old capital of Sikkim. Tumlong can be descried on a hill opposite, the monastery being a prominent landmark. A further three miles down is the Dikchu River, which is crossed, and the bank of the Teesta followed for two miles more, to the bungalow of Dikchu, perched above the river.

Dikchu, being only a trifle over two thousand feet above sea level, is the home of many insect pests, and in the summer, mosquito nets should be used at night.

To reach Singhik, the next day's march follows the Teesta all the way, climbing steadily. A mile from Dikchu bungalow will be seen the remains of a rubber plantation, planted for experimental purposes, which, however, did not prove a success. Several fine cane bridges are to be seen along this part of the Teesta, in their way works of genius in spanning the river with no other material than bamboos and lianas. Some of these bridges are of considerable length, and if a special thrill is desired, the traveller has only to cross one. Six miles from Dikchu, the Rong Rong River is crossed by a long suspension bridge, a couple of hundred feet or more above the river.

At the 21st milepost from Gantok, a bridge will be seen crossing the Teesta, on the way to Talung, the royal monastery of Sikkim, where many sacred relics are preserved. Singhik bungalow is at the 24th mile from Gantok.

These Teesta valley bungalows are very prettily set in gardens full of orchids and other flowering plants with fruit trees, especially oranges, where the elevation is not too high. From Singhik, a wonderful panorama of the snows is to be had on a clear day.

It is 13 miles to Chungtang, with the bungalow of Toong in between, at the 8th mile from Singhik. These two stages can, if necessary, be combined into one march, which can be done comfortably in one day.

The track from Singhik to Chungtang, is very beautiful, the path being high up on the valley side, with numerous waterfalls cascading across it. Vegetation is abundant.

Toong is at the 32nd mile from Gantok, and from here a steep drop of a mile brings the traveller to the bank of the Teesta, where there is a bridge.

At Chungtang, the Lachen and the Lachung Rivers meet to form the Teesta, at the 37th mile from Gantok. The Chungtang monastery is passed a mile before reaching the bungalow, the road crossing the Lachen River a little to the south of the resthouse. From this bridge, in bygone days, criminals were thrown into the river below, as a kind of trial by ordeal. If drowned, they were guilty ; if they emerged alive, their innocence was presumed.

A march of 13 miles along the Lachen River brings the traveller to the dak bungalow of that name. At certain parts of the road, the track is very precarious, overhanging the river. The whole way is a gradual ascent. Seven miles from Chungtang a path will be seen going off to the right to the hot springs of Taram Tsa Chu, which many Sikkimese and Tibetans visit for courses of baths and drinking the waters. After the 46th mile is passed, the scenery changes to the usual upland stony valleys.

Lachen is the headquarters of a Finnish Mission, the missionaries of which have done much in the way of teaching the local people home industries, in the form of weaving cloth and carpets, and apple culture. Apples from Lachen are very fine, and find a ready market in Kalimpong and Darjeeling. The bungalow is at the 50th milepost from Gantok. There is a local monastery, near which is housed the largest prayer wheel in Sikkim containing millions of repetitions of the sacred 'Om Mani' formula.

Thangu lies 13 miles beyond Lachen, the road still climbing and following the Lachen River. Two miles from the bungalow at Lachen, the Zemu River is crossed, this stream running from the glacier of the same name, which has its head in the snows of Kinchenjunga. Thangu is the northern most bungalow in Sikkim, and is the last on the road over the Donkya La. From here tents must be used for camping, and the riding ponies or mules sent back via Chungtang to meet the party at Yeumthang, in the Lachung Valley. Yaks may be hired both for riding and transport purposes.

From Thangu an ascent of 10 miles brings the traveller to Gyajong, the first camping ground. Though this march is short as far as mileage goes, it will be quite long enough for the tourist, as it is better to get somewhat acclimatised to the great heights before crossing the Donkya Pass, which is over 18000 feet above sea level. Firewood must be carried in sufficient quantities to last three days. None can be obtained after leaving Thangu. Gyajong is situated in a grassy plain at the 73rd milestone from Gantok, and tents should be pitched here. The yak drivers will point out the most sheltered spot, as they have done this trek many times.

All along this march, from Thangu to Yeumthang, most impressive views of the snows are to be had. It is advisable, however, not to attempt this trip too early in the year, as heavy snowdrifts may make travelling, if not impossible, at least very arduous. The road to Khamba Jong, in Tibet, will be seen going to the north from Gyajong. The road to the Donkya La follows the Yeum plain, an old lake bed, for about 8 miles, following the course of the Lachen.

Turning south at the end of the Yeum Lake, Chu Lhamo, the next camping ground, is close at hand. The tents should be pitched in the most sheltered spot available. From this camp the Donkya La is visible.

A climb of three miles brings the traveller to the summit, from which one of the finest views in Sikkim is obtainable. The scene is wild in the extreme, and the clarity of the atmosphere makes it possible to see for many miles across the jumbled mountain crests.

Mome Samdong, the next camping ground lies 8 miles beyond the Pass, the road descending all the way, passing en route the sources of the Lachung River, which is followed down. The camping ground cannot be missed as it is marked by some stone shelters used in the summer by the yakherdsmen.

Still descending, crossing the Sibu Chu on the way, a forest of pines is reached after about five miles, and the same distance on brings one to the resthouse of Yeumthang, where the ponies will be found waiting for the party.

A mile and a half from Yeumthang a track will be noticed, crossing a bridge, leading to some hot springs, where the traveller, if so inclined, may enjoy a bath. Another 2 miles of descent and the road opens on to a meadow, where a halt may be made for lunch. Lachung is five miles beyond this, over a somewhat rough track, subject in places to landslips, which may give difficulty in crossing.

Lachung is a big village for these parts, and is noted for its water driven series of prayer-wheels, which confer much spiritual merit on the place.

Chungtang, whence the traveller branched off on the outward journey to Thangu, is another 10 miles down the Lachung Valley, through a magnificent pine and rhododendron forest. Fine views are also to be had from many vantage spots of the road. Waterfalls drop across the road in many places.

The traveller returns to Gantok by the same route as covered when on the ontward trip. From Gantok he will follow the new motor road to Shamdong a distance of 12 miles. The first few miles, to the Rani Khola Bridge, are a steep descent. After crossing this the road descends very gradually until the bungalow is reached.

Between Shamdong and Singtam, 6 miles away, the road passes through some very fine orange groves, while the countryside is cultivated all the way. Singtam is a big bazaar village, with a Post Office. The river is crossed here by a good bridge, and another mile further on will be seen the bungalow of Sankakhola. A halt need not be made here, but the traveller should push on five miles to Rungpo, the Frontier Station between British India and Sikkim. The road follows the Teesta all the way from Singtam, rising and falling as the lie of the land demands.

Rungpo has a very fine dak bungalow, and is the centre of the orange trade of southern Sikkim.

Here, in the season, these fruits may be purchased very cheaply.

Still following the Teesta, the road runs on, passing Tarkhola, five miles from Rungpo to Melli, where a halt may be made for lunch. From here a short cut to Kalimpong may be taken, leading up through the forest at the back of the bungalow. If this is not taken, the traveller may push on to Teesta Bridge, where a car may be obtained for the last 10 miles, a steep climb, and rather uninteresting. If he prefers to ride, he should take the bridle path, which will be seen half a mile above the Teesta Bridge.

TOUR No. 3.

KALIMPONG to the Guicha La, *via* Pemayangtse and Jongri, returning *via* Phalut and Ghoom.

From Kalimpong, either the motor road or the shorter bridle path to Teesta Bridge should be taken. The motor road is advised, and the traveller should do this first ten miles by car, as from Kalimpong to Badamtam is a long march of 18½ miles. The kit should be sent off the day before. The road from Teesta Bridge runs through Teesta Bazaar, leaving the Peshok path at the Mangwa Bridge, where the latter will be seen turning off to the left up the hill. The traveller takes the right hand road, which follows the Teesta River as far as the junction of the Teesta and the Rungeet River. At this spot, in January, is held a festival called the Beni Mela, to which Hindoos from all over the Darjeeling District come to sacrifice. This junction of the waters is considered particularly holy. From Beni to Manjitar Bridge is 6 miles, and here there is a suspension bridge crossing into Sikkim. Leaving this on the right, a climb of a little over 3 miles brings the traveller to the Badamtam Dak Bungalow, 7½ miles below Darjeeling.

The next morning the traveller drops down the same road as that by which he came to the

Manjitar Bridge, which is left on the right, the path to the lower gardens of the Tukvar Tea Plantation being taken. Crossing a small stream, the Jepi Khola, and passing through the Tukvar garden for nearly 2 miles, the traveller comes to the Little Rungeet. Not quite half a mile beyond this is the Singla Bazaar.

Half a mile farther up the Rungeet River is the Police Outpost of Singla, where Frontier Passes must be shown, one copy being handed to the Police, the duplicate being retained for use on leaving Sikkim territory. Up to this place the path from Manjitar is more or less level, but from here to a couple of miles from the Chakung Bungalow is a steep pull up of 4 miles. Half a mile from Singla Police Station the path to the New Bazaar will be seen leading to the right. This is not taken.

Two miles along the level from the crest of the ridge brings the traveller to Chakung Bungalow from which fine views of the surrounding country are obtained.

Rinchenpong is reached after a trek of 12½ miles, beginning with a drop of 3 miles to the Ritu River. Thence a short pull up, and a mile or so of level brings one to a small stream, having forded which, a steep zig-zag ascent leads to the top of a ridge, marked by a Choten. Two miles steep down and another 2 miles climb finds the tourist at the junction of the two paths to Dentam and Rinchenpong. From here 2 miles level going brings the traveller to the Rinchenpong bungalow, from which very fine snow views are to be obtained in clear weather.

Rinchenpong is 12 miles from Pemayangtse, the day's march commencing with a 6 miles descent to the Kulhait Bridge over the river of the same name. Three miles down from Rinchenpong will be seen, in a clearing, several chotens and a large double dorje, or thunderbolt, carved on a flat stone. Crossing the Kulhait bridge, the junction, marked by a tea-shop, of Ligsip is reached. From here the road to Kewsing leaves the path to Pemayangtse.

Three and a half miles climb from Ligsip, brings the traveller to the busty of Dochen, where there is a small bazaar, and a further 2½ miles, still climbing, brings one to the spot whence the path to Pemayangtse Monastery leads off. The bungalow lies a short distance beyond and below this institution. The monastery, which has been described elsewhere, should be visited. From the bungalow glorious views are obtained, some of the finest in all Sikkim.

Riding animals cannot be taken beyond Pemayangtse; they must be sent from here to Phalut, *via* Dentam, where they should await the travellers return.

After Pemayangtse, tents must be used for shelter, these being preferable to the local houses, where such exist. All baggage must be carried by coolies. Sufficient provisions for these latter, as well as for the party, to last as far as Ghoom, must be carried along. Nothing can be purchased en route.

From Pamayangtse, the first day's march is to Yuksam. It may here be mentioned that though at this stage of the journey the actual mileage of each day's trek is small, the difficulties of the road, and the climbing that has to be done on foot, more than make up for the lessened distance covered.

The traveller starts off on the Dentam road, but after a very short distance, a small path will be seen going off to the right. This is taken, and the traveller descends 3 miles to the Rungbi River, whence a mile uphill and 2 miles more or less level, brings one to the Racha streamlet, 2 miles above which lies the village of Tingling. A halt may be made here, but it is advisable to push on to Yuksam, if possible. From Tingling no less than nine monasteries can be seen on the surrounding hills. These are Dubdi, Kangrhi, Simun, Talung, Tashiding, Pemayangtse, Sangachelling, Malli, and Katsupari.

From Tingling down to the Rathong is four miles steep descent, whence a further 6½ miles brings the traveller to Yuksam, the first 4 miles being a climb, and the remainder more or less level. Above the camping ground is the monastery of Dubdi, which should be visited. Yuksam is of special interest as it was here that the Tibetan lamas who were responsible for the introduction of Buddhism into Sikkim, first met and laid their plans for proselytising the people. From Yuksam onwards, the path lies through land untouched by human hand, the last traces of cultivation being left behind a mile from the village.

A march of about 7 miles, over an ill-defined track, and across small streams, crossed by crude bridges, and through heavy jungle brings the traveller to the camping ground of Nibi Rock, where a halt should be made for the night. This 7 miles will be found quite enough for the coolies with their loads.

An early start should be made next morning, for the very stiff march to Jongri. This begins with a four mile stretch of rough going to the Praig Chu, a fairly big stream crossed by a cane bridge. From the Praig River a very stiff climb of 8 miles through forest brings the traveller to the open country of Jongri. Three miles up from the Praig Chu is a clearing in the forest, and a halt for lunch may be made here. Three quarters of a mile along more or less level ground, and the tourist is at the camping ground of Jongri, marked by a rough yak-herds' hut. The view from the ridge at the back of this, where chotens will be noticed, is to be remembered. Jongri is 13200 feet above sea level.

All rations and baggage not required till the return journey from Jongri, should be left at that place, as all available men will be used for carrying wood for the last couple of marches to the Guichala, which are above the tree line, and on which no fuel is available locally.

From Jongri two miles through rhododendron bushes brings the traveller to the crossing of the Praig Chu, the road descending to this stream for about a mile. Four miles and a half from Jongri lies the camping ground of Wanglathang, a mile along the level from the Praig Chu and two and a half over very stony ground. From Wanglathang wonderful mountain scenery is visible.

At Wanglathang, the limit of the treeline, all available coolies should be loaded with firewood.

At the head of the valley of Wanglathang is a vast mass of debris, which has to be climbed. For the first 2 miles the path is more or less level when a half mile climb is necessary to negotiate the pile of debris referred to. After this for another half mile the track follows along the bank of a mountain lake, beyond which are two and a half miles strenuous climbing to a stony ridge, followed by a half mile through the boulders, and one and a half across the sands of the dried up lake beds. This place is called Chemthang. The foot of the Guicha La lies a mile and a half farther on, and here, in the most sheltered spot available, the tents should be pitched. The whole day's march is 7½ miles.

Next day, the trip consists of the visit to the top of the Guicha La, and only a couple of coolies for the tiffin basket and a rug or two and the cameras need be taken. Starting with a half mile of easy going, the path climbs precipitously for a mile or so to the summit of the Pass, whence a wonderful view of Kinchenjunga and the Talung Glacier, which has its roots here, is obtained. The Guicha is 16,600 feet above sea level. The return to the camp at the foot is made by the same route.

The return journey as far as Jongri is the same as the outward trip, and at that place the loads which have been left should be picked up.

The next day's march is to Churung Chu, possibly the most beautiful camping ground of the whole tour,placed in the midst of the rhododendron. It is reached by a path which traverses the west side of Kabru for a mile, after which there is a steep descent of another 3 miles to the Churung River, which is crossed by a wooden bridge. The camping ground is near the head of this.

Two miles climb brings the traveller to a spot called Bokta, where care should be exercised that the right path is taken. It is wise to include in the personnel some one who has been over this route before, thus avoiding error in choosing the correct track. 7½ miles of steep ups and downs across valleys brings one to the camping ground of Gamothang, another beauty spot. There is a stone herdsmen's hut at this place. To the opening of the valley to the south are descried the peaks of Pandim.

From Gamothang to the next camp at Migothang is 13 miles, fairly heavy marching. The first ¼ mile lies on level ground through the forest, then, following the stream, which is crossed after another ¼ mile, a stiff climb of another mile and a quarter brings the traveller to a ridge, passing the Lakshmi Pokri, a small lake in a depression, Still climbing, the Oma La is surmounted, from the top of which is a magnificent view of Everest and

Makalu. Crossing several more passes, the track, descending, passes the Tagmo Tso, where lunch may be eaten. From the Tagmo Tso to Migothang is 4½ miles, mostly through rhododendron forest.

Most of the march to the next camp, Nayathang, lies along the Nepal-Sikkim Frontier, a distance of about 14½ miles. The march begins with a climb to Lempharam, 13700 feet above sea level, and then drops to the Senden Pass. For the next eight miles the road switchbacks, with one or two steep descents and ascents. Numerous gots, or yak stations are passed, and the track ends with a drop down into Nayathang.

The next day's march takes the traveller back into the Darjeeling District, the Sikkim Frontier being crossed at Chiabanjam, 6 miles from Nayathang over rough going. Here the ponies may be picked up, and the remaining 6 miles to Phalut done on their backs. At Chiabanjam is a cairn marking the spot where Nepal, Sikkim and British India meet. From Phalut wonderful views are to be obtained.

Sandakphu lies 12½ miles from Phalut, and for the first mile the path zig-zags down the mountain side and continues on up and down for 3½ miles, whence the last view of Phalut is obtained. Eight miles of switchbacking, ending with a short climb, brings the traveller to the Sandakphu bungalow, near which is a good specimen of the prayer wall or mendong. The view from Sandakphu, on a clear morning, is considered by some to be one of the finest in the world.

Five miles brings the tourist to Kala Pokhri, the Black Pool, and another nine, the whole trek being of the switchback order, bring the Tonglu bungalow in sight. The going is fairly good most of the way. From Tonglu, Darjeeling is distinctly visible, as well as Kinchenjunga and the mountains in the same group. The next day, a long descent brings the traveller to Manibanjan, and after a corresponding ascent, through Simana, the tourist has arrived in Jorepokri, where a halt will be made in the dak bungalow, a mile and a half above the village of Sukiapokri, whence it is only a march of 7 miles to Ghoom or Jorebungalow, passing en route the well known picnic spot of Ghoom Rock. A halt for the night may be made at either of the two hotels in Ghoom, the Pines, or the Balaclava.

From Ghoom the road runs more or less level for three miles, and then gradually drops to the 6th milepost from the village, where the broad road to the abandoned cantonment of Takdah will be noticed leading off to the right. The path to Rangiroon Forest bungalow will also be seen running away down to the left. Continuing on the road remains broad for another two miles, when it becomes a very good pony track. Lopchu dak bungalow is passed at the 10th milepost from Ghoom, and a descent of another 7 miles through forest and through the Peshok Tea Plantation brings the traveller to the resthouse of Peshok.

Next morning, passing View Point ½ mile below the bungalow, whence a fine view of the meeting of the Teesta and the Rungit may be had, the road drops fairly steeply to the Mangwa Bridge, three miles lower down, and from here the path taken on the outward journey may be descried going off to the left. Crossing this bridge, the traveller passes through Teesta Bazaar, and crossing Teesta Bridge, has the choice of two roads to Kalimpong. The bridle path, climbing steeply to three miles from Kalimpong, is the best for riding, while if a car is used the broad motor road will be taken. From Teesta Bridge a ride of 2 miles brings the traveller to Gielle Khola Station, on the Darjeeling Himalayan Railway, should he not wish to revisit Kalimpong.

FRONTIER PASSES.

1. Europeans visiting Sikkim and Tibet are required to carry passes and unless provided with passes will not be allowed beyond the Darjeeling frontier. Passes are issued by Deputy Commissioner, Darjeeling, and Political Officer in Sikkim, Gantok, Sikkim.

2. Passes for the bungalows on this list are issued as follows:—

Nos. 1-40 by Deputy Commissioner Darjeeling.

Nos. 42-47 by Executive Engineer, Darjeeling Division.

Nos. 48-56 by Political Officer, Gantok, Sikkim.

3. All applications made to the above officers for passes should be addressed to them as such, and not by name. Those for the Political Officers should be addressed to the Agency Office, Gantok, Sikkim; those for the Deputy Commissioner to the Deputy Commissioner's Office, Darjeeling; those for the Executive Engineer, to the Executive Engineer's Office, Darjeeling.

Travellers' Bungalows in Darjeeling District, Sikkim and Tibet.

No.	Place.	Distances in Miles.	Height in feet above M. S. L.	Bed room
1	Senchal (old)	... 6 from Darjeeling	... 8,000	4
	Senchal (new)	... 6 " "	... 8,000	2
2	Rangiroon	... 7 " "	... 5,700	2
3	Badamtam	... 7 " "	... 2,500	2
4	Mirik	...25 " " 12 from Jorepokri	... 5,000	2
5	Lopchu	...15 " " 4 " Pashoke	... 5,300	2
6	Kalimpong	...28 " " via Pashoke and Bridle path and 23 via Rungit and Bridle path	... 4,100	4
7	Rississum	...12 from Kalimpong, 4 from Pedong	... 6,410	3
8	Jorepokri	...13 from Darjeeling, 10 from Tonglu	... 7,400	2
9	Tonglu	...10 from Jorepokri, 14 from Sandakphu	... 10,074	2
10	Sandakphu	...14 from Tonglu, 12 from Phalut	... 11,929	2
11	Phalut	...12 from Sandakphu, 17 from Dentam	... 11,811	2
12	Dentam	...17 from Phalut, 11 from Pamionchi 13 from Rinchinpong	... 4,500	2
13	Pamionchi	...11 from Dentam, 10 from Rinchinpong	... 6,920	2
14	Rinchinpong	...10 from Pamionchi, 13 from Chakung, 13 from Dentam	... 6,300	2

No.	Place.	Distance in Miles.	Height in feet above M. S. L	Bed room
15	Chakung	...13 from Rinchinpong, 20 from Darjeeling via Singla Bazar & Raman-bridge, 13 from Badamtam ...	5,100	2
16	Rungpo	...11 from Melli, 9 from Pakyong, 5 from Sankokhola ...	1,200	4
17	Sankokhola (Bardang)	... 5 from Rangpo, 18 from Kalimpong ...	1,400	3
18	Shamdang (Middle camp)	... 7 from Sankokhola, 9 from Gangtok by short cut—12 by cart road ...	2,300	2
19	Gangtok	... 9 from Shamdang by short cut—12 by cart road, 51 to 63 from Darjeeling according to route followed: quickest route via Melli Chhapar bridge and Badamtam ...	5,800	5
20	Pakyong	... 9 from Rungpo, 11 from Gangtok, 14 from Pedong, 6 from Rorathang ...	4,700	2
21	Kyozing (Soshing)	...10 from Pamionchi, 10 from Rinchinpong 5 from Ligsip ...	6,000	2

No.	Place.	Distance in Miles.	Height in feet above M. S. L.	Bed room
22	Temi	...10 from Kyozing, 11 from Namchi, 14 from Shamdang and Rungpo ...	5,000	2
23	Song	...12 from Temi, 15 from Gangtok ...	4,500	2
24	Namchi	...11 from Badamtam, 14 from Chakung ...	5,200	2
25	Ari	...12 from Pakyong, via Rhenock, 8 from Pedong	4,700	3
26	Rhenock	... 3 from Ari, 5 from Pedong ...	3,200	1
27	Rongli	... 9 from Sedonchen, 15 from Rungpo, 13 from Pakyong, 4 from Ari ...	2,700	2
28	Sedonchen	...13 from Ari, 9 from Rongli ...	6,500	1
29	Gnatong	... 9 from Sedonchen ...	12,300	2
30	Kupup	... 4 from Gnatong, 3 from Summit of Jelap-La, 9 from Pusum ...	13,000	2
31	Pusum (Karponang)	...10 from Gangtok ...	9,500	2
32	Changu	...11 from Pusum ...	12,600	2
33	Dikchu (Riatdong)	...13 from Gangtok, 11 from Singhik ...	2,150	2
34	Singhik	...11 from Dikchu ...	4,600	2
35	Toong	... 8 from Singhik ...	4,800	2
36	Chungtang	... 5 from Toong ...	5,350	2

No.	Place.	Distance in Miles.	Height in feet above M. S. L.	Bed room
37	Lachen	...13 from Chungtang ...	8,800	2
38	Thangu	...13 from Lachen ...	12,800	2
39	Lachung	...10 from Chungtang ...	8,800	2
40	Yumtang	... 8 from Lachung ...	11,700	4
41	Pedong	...12 from Kalimpong, 4 from Rississum 5 from Rhenock ...	4,900	6
42	Pashoke	...17 from Darjeeling, 4 from Lopchu 3 from Tista Bridge ...	2,600	4
43	Tista Bridge	...23 from Darjeeling, 3 from Pashoke, 6 from Kalimpong 11 from Badamtam, 5 from Reang ...	710	3
44	Reang	... 5 from Tista Bridge, 4 from Berrik (D. H. Ry. Rest house) ...	625	4
45	Birrik	...10 from Tista Bridge, 5 from Kalijhora ...	900	2
46	Kalijhora	... 5 from Berrik, 16 from Siliguri ...	550	3
47	Melli	... 5 from Kalimpong, 11 from Badamtam and Rungpo 3 from Tista Bridge ...	800	2
48	Champithang	...12 from Yatung, 12 from Changu ...	13,090	2
49	Yatung	...16 from Kupup, 12 from Gautsa ...	9950	2

No.	Place.	Distance in Miles.	Height in feet above M. S. L.	Bed room
50	Gautsa	...16 from Pharijong	... 12300	2
51	Pharijong	...21 from Tuna	... 14500	2
52	Tuna	...12 from Dochen	... 14980	2
53	Dochen	...12 from Kala	... 14900	2
54	Kala	...14 from Samoda	... 14700	2
55	Samoda	...14 from Kangma	... 14400	2
56	Kangma	...14 from Savgong	... 13900	2
57	Saugong	...14 from Gyantse	... 13800	2
58	Gyantse	...14 from Saugong	... 13600	3

CAMPING GROUND

No.	Place.	Distance in Miles.	Height in feet above M. S. L.
1	Gyajong	...10 from Thango	... 15750
2	Tso Lhama	...13 from Gyajong	... 17000
3	Mome Samdong	11 from Tso Lhamo, 10 from Yeumthang	... 15000
4	Tingling	... 7 from Pema Yangtse	... 6000
5	Yuksan	...10½ from Tingling	... 6000
6	Nibi Rock	... 7 from Yuksan	... 8000
7	Jongri	...12½ from Nibi Rock	... 13140
8	Wanglathang.	...4½ from Jongri	... 13500

No.	Place.	Distance in Miles.	Height in feet above M. S. L.	Bed room
9	Guicha La (foot of)	... 2½ from top of Pass 7½ from Wanglathang	... 15000	
10	Chorung Chu	... 5 from Jongri	... 12100	
11	Gamothang	... 9½ from Churung Chu	... 12550	
12	Migothang	...13 from Gamothang	... 13000	
13	Nayathang	...14 from Phalut 12½ from Migothang	... 11800	

Nos. 1-3 are on the Donkya Route Nos. 4-13, on the Guicha La Route via Phalut.

4 The bungalows are available only to persons provided with passes. A separate pass must be obtained for each occupant or party of occupants for each bungalow whether going or returning. Persons occupying bungalows without passes will be required to pay double fees, provided accommodation be available.

1 **Fees**—Eight annas for each person for occupation during the day up-to a maximum charge of *six rupees.* Two rupees per night for each occupant. In case of Senchal (new) & Kalimpong the charge for each occupant is Rs. 3/- & 2/- per night respectively up-to a maximum of Rs. 10/-.

1. In the case of Senchal (old), Rangiroon and Badamtam the charge for occupation, by day only, is eight annas for each person, up-to a maximum of ***six rupees.***
2. Passes may be cancelled by the local authorities without payment of compensation.
3. A refund of bungalow fees is not allowed after the issue of a pass, unless it is cancelled.
4. Passes must be made over to the Chowkidar in charge.
5. Fees are payable in advance to the Political Officer in Sikkim, Gantok, Deputy Commissioner or Executive Engineer, Darjeeling, on the submission of the application for the pass.
6. Government officers on duty are allowed to occupy the bungalows in the Darjeeling District and Tibet free of charges. In Sikkim they are charged full rates if they occupy for more than 7 days.
7. Out station cheques in payment of fees should include four annas for every twenty five rupees, as discount.

II. Furniture etc.— Beds, Tables, Chairs, Lamps with wicks, Candlesticks, Crockery, Glass and Kitchen utensils are provided at each bungalow, cutlery is supplied in Sikkim and Tibet bungalows, also mattresses in bungalows above 7000 feet, (See V (ii) below)

2. Visitors must take their own Bedding, Linen, Candles, Oil for Lamps, Provisions, and in the Darjeeling District, Cutlery.

III. Provision etc.— Ordinary bazaar supplies are obtainable at Jorepokri, Dentam, Pamionchi, Kalimpong, Tista Bridge, Pedong, Namchi, Pakyong, Rhenock, Rongli, Rungpo, Gangtok and Singtam, near Sankokhola, Yatung and Gyantse.

2. Firewood is provided free of charge on the Nepal Frontier Road bungalows. At Kalimpong four annas a maund. The charges for firewood in the Sikkim bungalows are notified in the bungalows and are payable before delivery of the wood whether used by travellers themselves or by their servants, coolies, &c. In most of the Tibet bungalows Yakdung is the only fuel locally obtainable.

IV. Servants.—1 A sweeper can be hired at Kalimpong, Jorepokri, Tista Bridge, Rungpo, Sankokhola, Gangtok, Pakyong, Namchi, Rhenock, Rongli, Dentam and Senchal, Yatung & Gyantse.

2. Elsewhere travellers must take sweepers with them, and no pass will be issued except on this condition.

3. There is no resident Khansamah at any bungalow.

V. Situation.—

(i) On the Nepal Frontier Road ... ... Nos. 1 to 11
(ii) In Sikkim ... ... „ 12 to 41
(iii) On the road from Kalimpong to the Jelap Pass „ 26 to 31 & 42
(iv) On the Tista Valley Road ... ... „ 16 to 18 & 44 to 47
(v) On the road from Gangtok to theNathu La Pass „ 32 & 33
(vi) On the Road from Gangtok along the upper Tista & in the Lachen & Lachung Valleys „ 34 to 41
(vii) 23, 24 and 25 are on the Darjeeling Gangtok Melli Road across the hills (via Badamtam Rungit Bazar.)
(viii) 21 is on the Pedong Gangtok Road via Rishi suspension Bridge.
(ix) 7 is on the Daling Road to the Plains.
(x) On the Gyantse Road „ 48 to 58

Agriculture, 81,
Algarah, 87,
Alukthang, 121,
Amo Chu, 96,
Animism, 8,
Animists, 8,
Apples, 111,
Ari, 90,
Arts & Crafts, 83,

Badamtam, 116,
Baggage of servants, 37,
Bamboos, 19,
Bardang, 114,
Bathing, 66,
Bazaar supplies, 44,
Bedding, 41,
Beggars, 64,
Beni Mela, 116,
Berrik, 131,
Bhutan Durbar House, 87,
Bibliography, 56, 74,
Bidang Lake, 94,
Blisters, 54,
Bogle, 101,
Bokta, 123,
Books, 56,
Boots, 54,
Bread, 46,
Bridle Paths, 21,
British Trade Agent, 14,96,
Butterflies, 21,

Cairns, 95,
Camp Equipment, 64,
Campbell, Sir. R. 12
Candles, 43,
Cane Bridges, 109,
Carrying Chairs, 59,
Cemetery, 93,
Chakung, 117,
Champithang, 104
Chandra Nursery, 90,
Changu, 105,
,, Lake, 105,
Charteris Hospital, 80,
Chemthang, 122,
Cheques, 52, 84,
Chiabanjam, 124,
China, 12,
Chinese Customs Post, 95,
Chits, 53,
Chola Ridge, 4,
Chomolhari, 5, 95,
Chotens, 17,
Chu Lhamo, 112,
Chu-mik-chan, 89,
Chukya, 99,
Chumbi Valley, 96,
Chungtang, 110,
Churang, 123,
Churang River, 123,
Cicadas, 21,
Claude White, J. 2,
Climbing, 71,
Clothing, 39,
Coolies, 36, 62,
Curios, 23,
Curio shops, 23, 84,
Currency notes, 52,

Dak bungalows, 30,
" " fees, 30,
" " furniture, 31,
" " heights, 128.
" " list of, 128,
" " rules, 127,
Dak Runners, 92,
Dalai Lama, 14, 87,
Dandies, 59,
Darjeeling, 76,
Darjeeling, Himalayan Railway, 126,
Deforestation, 7,
Dejong, 1,
Demonstration Farm, 81,
Dentam. 118,
Deolo 83,
Depons 50,
Derby Downs 93
Desgodins, Father 89,
Detailed Tours 86,
Dikchu 108,
Dik River 108,
Dochen (Sikkim). 118,
Dochen (Tibet) 101,
Doctors, 59,
Donka Monastery, 97,
Donkya La, 112,
Dooars, 41,
Dorje, Raja S. T. 87,
Dotha Plain, 97,
" Waterfall, 97,
Double marches, 49,
Douenil, Monsignor, 89,
Dried Fish, 101,
Drinking Water, 45,
Dubdi Monastery, 120,
Durpindara, 85,

Electric torches, 43,
Everest, 2,
Expenses, 68,
Exposure Photographic, 63,
Extra kit, servants 68,

Face creams, 66,
Feet, Care of, 54,
Finnish Missions. 111,
Fishing Rules, 78,
Fishing Tours, 77,
Flora, 19,
Frescoes, 16,
Frontier Commission, 13,
" Passes, 28, 90,
" " , fees, 28,
" " , Sikkim, 29,
" " , Tibet, 29,

Gamothang, 123,
Gantok, 106,
Gautsa, 97,
Gazelle, 100,
Ghoom Rock, 125,
Giagong, 111,
Glare Glasses, 62,
Gnatong, 93,
Gots, 124,
Government Coolies, 38,
Graham, Dr. J. A. 83,
Guicha La, 122,
Gurkhas, 11,
Guru, 100,
Gyantse, 103,
Gyajong, 111,

Heart subjects, 70,

Himalayan Hotel, 32, 50,
Hinduism, 15,
Honesty, of coolies, 36,
Hooker, Sir J. 12,
Hospitals, 60,
Hot Springs, 103, 110,
Hram Lake, 100,
Hurricane lanterns, 43,

Incense Tree, 89,
Interpreters, 61,
Iron, 42,

Jaldakha River, 94,
Jelep La, 94,
Jeluk, 92,
Jepi Khola, 117,
Jongri, 121,
Jongpens, 141,
Jorebungalow, 125,
Jorepokhri, 125,

Kabru, 123,
Kala, 101,
,, Lake, 101,
Kalapokri, 125,
Kalijhora, 77,
Kalimpong, 72, 79,
,, , climate, 80,
,, , Mela, 82,
Kalimpong, Mission, 83,
,, , Mission Indusries, 83,
,, , Water supply, 80,
,, , Road Station, 79,
Kamparab, 98,
Kangma, 102,
Kanghri Monastery, 120,
Kargyu Monastery, 104,
Karponang, 105,
Kartok Monastery, 107,
Katsupari Monastery, 120,
Kazis, 8,
Kewsing, 118,
Khamba Jong, 112,
Khatmandu, 12,
Kinchenjunga, 2,
Kings of the Quarters, 17,
Kodaks, 63,
Kulhait Bridge, 118,
Kupup, 94,
Kyang, 100,

Lachen, 111,
Lachen River, 3, 110,
Lachung, 113,
Lachung River, 3, 110, 113,
Lakshmi Pokri, 123,
Lamaism, 15,
Lamaist Elements, 18,
Lamas, 10,
Lamps, 43,
Langram, 95,
Leeches, 58,
Lempharam, 124,
Lepchas, 7,
Letters, 51,
,, of introduction, 32,
Ligsip, 118,
Limbuana, 11,
Lingmathang, 97,
Lingtam, 91,
Lingtu, 13, 92,

Little Rungeet River, 117,
Lopchu, 126,

Macfarlane Memorial Church, 83,
Makalu, 123,
Maharaja of Sikkim, 11,
Malli Monastery, 120,
Mangwa Bridge, 116,
Manibanjam, 125,
Manjitar Bridge, 116,
Maps, 70,
Marches, 47,
Maria Busty, 89,
Marwaries, 9,
Masks, 66,
Mattresses, 42,
Medical Attendance, 59,
Medicines, 55,
Melli, 115,
Mendong, 18,
Migothang, 124,
Mileage, 72,
Milestones, 102,
Milk, 45,
Mome Samdong, 113,
Monasteries, 15,
Money, 52,
Mosquito Nets, 42,
Mosquitos, 42, 59,
Moths, 21,
Motor hire, 33,
,, Roads, 33, 106,
Mountain sickness, 60,
Muleteers, 38, 62
Murray Road, 87,

Nagartse, 102,
Nathu La, 105,
Nayathang, 124,
Nepal, 124,
Nepalese, 7,
New Bazaar, 117,
Nibi Rock, 120,
Nim La, 94,
Nyang Chu, 102,

Old Yatung, 95,
Oil, Kerosine, 43,
Oma La, 123,
Orange Groves, 109,
,, Markets, 114,
Orchids, 109,

Pakyong, 106,
Palkhor Choide, 103,
Parties, Composition of, 55
Pay, advances of, 52, 67,
Pedong, 89,
Pemayangtse, 15, 118, 120
Penlong La, 108,
Peshok, 126,
Pests, 58,
Phalut, 124,
Pharijong, 98,
Phema, 96,
Photography, 63,
Pibithang, 96,
Plateau, of Tibet, 5,
Post Offices, 51,
Praig Chu, 120,
Prayer Flags, 18,
,, Wheels, 17,
Presents, 49,
Priests, 10,
Pun-sum-thang, 98,

Rainfall, 3,
Rangiroon, 125,
Rathong River, 120,
Red Idol Gorge, 103,
Religion, 15,
Rhenock, 90,
Rhododendrons, 19,
Riding Animal, 37,
Rilli River, 80,
Rinchengong, 96,
Rinchenpong, 117,
Ringkingpong, 83,
Rishi Bridge, 90,
Rississum, 88,
Ritu River, 117
Roman Cath. Mission, 89,
Rong, 7,
Rong Rong River, 108,
Rongli, 90,
Rongni Rivet, 106,
Rorathang Bridge, 107,
Roro River, 106,
Rungeet River, 3, 116,
Rungbi River, 119,
Rungpo, 114,
Rungpo River, 107

St. Andrew's Colonial Homes, 83,
St. Josheph's Convent, 85,
Samoda, 102,
Sandakphu, 124,
Sangachalling Monas, 120,
Saugong, 103,
Scarves, ceremonial, 50,
Schools, 83,
Scots Mission, 83,
Scott. Hon. Miss M. 106,
Sedonchen, 91,
Servants, 34,
,, , pay of, 34,
,, , mounting, 37,
Sevoke, 4,
Shap-pes, 14,
Sharabthang, 105,
Sheep, wild, 22,
Sherpas, 8,
Shobra Shubra, 99,
Shooting, 22,
,, , centres, 77,
,, , rules, 22,
Shooting and Fishing Club, 22,
Sibu River, 113,
Sikkim, 1,
,, , flora, 19,
,, , internal affairs,12,
Siliguri, 79,
Simana, 125,
Simun Monastery, 120,
Singelela Ridge, 4,
Singhik, 109,
Singla Bazaar, 117,
Sirdard 61,
Sleeping Bags, 42,
Small Change, 53,
Snow Blindness, 62,
Sores, on animals, 49,
Specimen Tours, 72,
Sport, 21,
Storeboxes, 45,
Stores, 43,
Stoves, 43,
Sukiapokri, 125,
Superstition, 10,
Suram Se, 106,

Tagmo Lake, 124,
Takdah, 125,
Talung Glacier, 122,
„ Monastery, 109, 120,
Tang La, 99,
Tantric Cult, 16,
Tarkhola, 115,
Tashiding monastery, 120,
Taylor, Miss Annie, 95,
Teesta Bazaar, 116,
„ Bridge, 116,
„ River 3,
„ Valley, 113,
Telegrams, 51,
Telegraph Offices, 51,
Telephoto lenses, 64,
Temples 17,
Terai, 12,
Thangu, 111,
Thri Sron de Tsan, 11,
Tibet, 5, 14,
Tibetan Mint 97,
Tibetan Trade Agent, 14,
Tiffin coolie, 36,
Tingling, 119,
Tips, 53,
Tobacco, 46,
Toilet preparations, 66,
Tonglu, 125,
Toong, 110,
Touring, 24 at seq,
„ centres, 32,
Transport, 36, 48,
„ rates, 38,
Tsalu, 101,
Tuko La, 93,
Tumlong Jong, 108,
Tuna, 99,

Underclothing, 41,

View Point, 126,

Walking, 37,
„ Parties, 68,
Wanglathang, 121,
Washing of clothes, 39, 49
Wildfowl, 100,
Wool Trade, 81,

Yakdung, 98,
Yatung, 96,
Yeumthang, 113,
Younghusband Mission, 99,
Yuksam, 119,

Zemu River, 111.